# CAREERS TO PRESERVE OUR SHRINKING WORLD

*WORKING AND
LIVING WITH
APPROPRIATE TECHNOLOGY*

THE CONSERVATION-ORIENTED techniques called appropriate technology are creating important new jobs for the future. This book explores the fields in which appropriate technology is being introduced, like recycling waste into energy and fresh water, energy-conservative architecture, aquaculture of foods, environment-conscious farming, and stewardship of wilderness areas. New jobs will be opening up in these fields; this book will help readers to prepare in time for the future.

*Also by Robert V. Doyle*

Your Career in Interior Design

# CAREERS TO PRESERVE OUR SHRINKING WORLD

*WORKING AND LIVING WITH APPROPRIATE TECHNOLOGY*

## by ROBERT V. DOYLE

*JULIAN MESSNER*
NEW YORK

Library of Congress Cataloging in Publication Data

Doyle, Robert V., 1916–
    Careers to preserve our shrinking world.

    Bibliography: p.
    Includes index.
    Summary: Explores the fields in which appropriate
technology, any technology used for the common
good which conserves the diminishing store of
natural resources, is being introduced.
    1. Technology—Juvenile literature. 2. Energy
conservation—Juvenile literature. 3. Environmental protection—Juvenile literature. 4. Conservation of natural resources—Juvenile literature.
[1. Technology. 2. Energy conservation. 3. Environmental protection. 4. Conservation of
natural resources] I. Title.
T48.D687        333.7′2        81–1880
ISBN 0–671–34046–8        AACR2

# CONTENTS

*To Robert Allen, M.D.,*
*and colleagues*
*—with gratitude*

# ACKNOWLEDGMENTS

THIS BOOK came alive while we were attending seminars on life-style and energy source alternatives sponsored by the California Office of Appropriate Technology (OAT). These brown-bag lunch meetings brought together people from all over the nation and world who shared the thought that a better way must be found for travelers on Spaceship Earth to survive and flourish.

We will always remember with warmth the amiability of the OAT staff who made us feel at home within their circle. These include Kirk Marckwald, then executive director of

OAT; Wade Rose, project manager of the waste-water disposal project; Stephanie Pincetl, who put the first OAT library together; and Dianne Winner, who handled the office chores.

As the OAT staff grew, Sim Van der Ryn, who was state architect at that time, Wilson Clark, assistant to the governor on planning issues, and Bill Press, director of the governor's Office of Planning and Research, under whose jurisdiction OAT blossomed, all were most friendly and supportive to us in our research. Ken Smith, leader of the OAT design team also was helpful.

Gigi Coe, who succeeded Kirk Marckwald as executive director, has assisted us in many ways as we struggled to tie all ends together. Bob Judd, OAT director, has been free with his friendly consideration for our project. Janice Jacobson, OAT librarian, has cheerfully put up with our prying into her files, papers, and books.

And we do not want to forget all the other kind OAT people with whom we have come in contact during the past few years. Not the least of these are Kate Janney and Richard Wenn, who found time during their busy itinerary to show us through the OAT New Possibilities Show traveling trailer.

Most of all, however, we want to thank Judy Michalowski, OAT program coordinator, for her steady flow of information and indulgent acceptance of our aims and viewpoints. It was Judy who answered our first queries in a fashion that made our project seem feasible and worthwhile. Judy and her husband, state architect Barry Wasserman, hold a special place in our heart.

Inspiration nourished by OAT led to our meeting with other appropriate technology activists. These include Ray and Judy Tretheway, solar believers: Bill Hollibaugh and Mark Goldes, entrepreneurs; Rosemary Menninger, community garden coordinator, and Paolo Soleri, architectural innovator; Margaret Morgan and Linda Cohen, from the Big Apple; and Valerie Pope, who has saved a little of San Bernardino from total decay.

Charles Little, Robert Kourick, Andrew Atkeison, and Reny Slay, from the Farallones Rural Center, who made the lovely hills near Occidental seem "at home."

Neil Seldman and Dan Knapp, recyclers, and Dominick Mendola, waste-water magician, who showed us that there is much of value in garbage and sewage.

Nancy Simpson, who well may have begun a new cottage industry in raising silkworms; Denis Hayes, who will continue to be the guiding "solar light;" and Claire Dedrick, California Public Utilities Commissioner, who made us believe that the light will always be guarded and preserved.

John Olmstead, through his active participation, and B. T. Collins, that intrepid leader of the California Conservation Corps, who have shown us open trails for all to enjoy and cherish.

Bill Mollison, from "Down Under," who carries with him a dream that one hopes will someday be realized.

And Robert Paul Mayer, whose research assistance was timely and invaluable.

All of these good people made the work on this book a most pleasurable undertaking. The author is eternally grateful.

We wish to add here that the book itself would not have been possible without the help of two remarkable, patient women: Jane Steltenpohl, Julian Messner's editor of books for young adults; and my wife, Margie. Only they knew the difficult circumstances under which this work was accomplished. My thanks will never reach the high level of my appreciation.

## 12  ACKNOWLEDGMENTS

The author and publisher are also grateful to the following for permission to excerpt and reprint copyrighted material in this book:

ACADEMIC PRESS, INC., for excerpts from *Wood as an Energy Resource* by David A. Tillman, Academic Press, Inc., 1978.

CHICAGO TRIBUNE-NEW YORK NEWS SYNDICATE for excerpts from a column by Jimmy Breslin, "Shelter for the Wealthy," February 16, 1979. Copyright © 1979 by Jimmy Breslin. Reprinted by permission of The Sterling Lord Agency, Inc.

HARPER & ROW for excerpts from *Small Is Beautiful: Economics as if People Mattered* by E. F. Schumacher, 1973.

HOUGHTON MIFFLIN for excerpts from *Silent Spring* by Rachel Carson. Copyright © 1962 by Rachel L. Carson. Reprinted by permission of the publisher, Houghton Mifflin Company.

INTERIORS for excerpts from an article by Olga Gueft, "Planned like a City," December, 1979.

THE MELANESIAN COUNCIL OF CHURCHES, Lae, PNG, for excerpts from *The Liklik Buk: A Rural Development Handbook for Papua New Guinea.*

NEW AMERICAN LIBRARY for a quote by William A. Caldwell from his book, *How to Save Urban America*, 1973.

RODALE PRESS for excerpts from *Poisoned Power: The Case Against Nuclear Power Plants* by John W. Gofman and Arthur R. Tamplin, 1979; also: excerpts from "Cole's Column" by John Cole, *New Shelter*, May, 1980.

TAGARI PUBLISHERS for quotes by Bill Mollison from his book, *Permaculture II: Practical Design for Town and Country in Permanent Agriculture*, 1979; and for quotes from *The Liklik Buk* and Virgil.

# INTRODUCTION

*MAN IS SMALL,*
*AND, THEREFORE,*
*SMALL IS BEAUTIFUL.*

E. F. SCHUMACHER

IN 1973 the oil embargo and subsequent shortages and price increases in gasoline and heating oil made Americans aware of our dependence on foreign suppliers. Before this time, writer-scientists like Rachel Carson had been criticizing the chemical industries for their role in slowly destroying nature's balance. Others, including the New Alchemists from Cape Cod, having read Carson, became active in a search for new technologies. Economist E. F. Schumacher wrote and talked about technologies more appropriate to human life on the planet. Urban planners started to take a closer look at priorities and the citizens' role in establishing programs and projects for their own benefit.

In the spring of 1976, the administration of California Gov. Edmund G. Brown, Jr., established the Office of Appropriate Technology (OAT) in Sacramento. The small staff of four began a low-keyed effort to educate interested people in state government through a series of seminars designed to open up lines of communication in such innovative techniques—new at that time—as solar energy applications, solid-waste recycling, waste-water treatment, agricultural land conservation, transportation, forestry, and home insulation.

Governor Brown, in creating OAT, charged it with developing technologies ". . . which are less harmful to people and the environment than the technologies of the past." In this vein, OAT has assisted and advised the governor and encouraged state agencies to develop and implement less costly and less energy-intensive technologies in many fields.

Similar efforts have been attempted in other sections of the country by governmental agencies. A bulletin issued by the Citizens' Energy Project out of Washington, D.C., says, "In the fall of 1976, the Community Services Administration provided an initial grant of $3 million to create a National Center for Appropriate Technology (NCAT) to develop and implement technologies appropriate to low-income communities."

Among its first actions, the Center—located in Butte, Montana—appointed a number of outreach workers to launch a dozen regional AT newsletters. Other programs were started in various cities and states. The state governments of New York, Kansas, and Hawaii have made attempts, so far unsuccessful, to begin Offices of Appropriate Technology patterned after the California OAT version.

We have covered many nationwide AT activities in this volume. However, we feel AT received its foremost impetus in California OAT seminars, where AT people from around the world came to share experiences and to offer helpful suggestions for working within government programs. In preparing this book we have attended many OAT seminars in California during the past five years, as well as visiting projects and talking with AT people in other parts of the country. We are convinced that what is happening now in these places will spread throughout the country.

We have found that AT people *live* AT. They work under AT standards; nothing else will satisfy their beliefs. We became acquainted with many appropriate technology activists who took part in the seminars. We studied with them the many ways for the world to evolve into an environmentally sound spaceship called Earth. We learned that we were all passengers, with but one vehicle—this beautiful "small world."

AT people feel that if a technology is not appropriate to the common good, if it does not conserve the natural resources, it has no place on the spaceship. They have found that the natural nonrenewable resources of this small world were being disposed of as quickly as they were made available to an eager, wasteful people.

Worse, not only were the resources squandered; the residue was collecting at an alarming rate. Toxic fluids were found in freshwater tables, in the aquatic food chain. Clouds of noxious gases choked the cities and gathered in the foothills. Solid wastes overflowed landfill sites. Sewage tainted some of the world's most beautiful lakes and rivers.

AT activists preach earnestly against these evils. They take a special interest in helping people improve their quality of life through self-reliance. Quietly they teach ways to survive without dependence on oil and public utilities; how to heat a home without natural gas or electricity; how to derive all the energy needed from the original source: the sun.

As the last two decades of the century unfold, more and more people will become attracted to AT. New industries in low technology will arise as new inventions are perfected. As we have met and talked with a number of these new AT people, we have seen career opportunities becoming available.

We saw work in progress where raw sewage is converted into pure, potable water in which fish and shrimp grow plump and tasty. We witnessed first accounts of building rehabilitation on the Lower East Side of New York City.

These experiences and more we pass on to you.

Young people entering the career world should be aware of the new world of appropriate technology that is opening before us. It is the way of the future. You can be part of it.

And so, welcome to a new world. A small but beautiful world. The only world we have.

We hope you will help keep it alive through appropriate technology.

*R.V.D.*
1981

# CHAPTER 1
# WHAT IS APPROPRIATE TECHNOLOGY?



RICHARD WENN and Kate Janney pull into the empty fairgrounds parking lot. It is early morning, before the crowds will come. Kate is at the wheel of the truck; on its door is the blue-and-gold symbol of the state of California. They are hauling a heavy, dual-wheel trailer that resembles a carnival wagon.

"New Possibilities Show," proclaims a brightly painted sign on the trailer's side. "IDEAS—TOOLS—PRODUCTS" —the bright lettering and colorful design scream for attention. It is the California Office of Appropriate Technology

(OAT) traveling trailer exhibit, taken to county fairs, schools, ballparks, or anywhere a crowd may be scheduled to gather.

Richard and Kate and the New Possibilities Show visit wherever people request information about alternative sources of energy; about recycling and conservation; about gardening and urban forestry. They cover the state, from Oregon to the Mexican border, answering questions, demonstrating methods.

On the trailer's rear is a solar hot-water collector; inside are all the latest tools for protecting the environment; there are reams of current literature about solar energy, wind power, alcohol conversion.

When a wide side door is swung open, a printed message comes into view:

### What Is Appropriate Technology?

A technology is a tool, a means to an end. The purpose of using it is to satisfy human needs such as food, shelter, health, a clean environment, and a sense of community. To decide whether a particular technology is an appropriate tool, ask these questions:

Is this technology necessary?

Will it satisfy basic needs?

Will it use, as much as possible, renewable resources?

Will it make good use of whatever nonrenewable resources it needs?

Have the size and design been matched to the task?

Has the impact on the environment been kept to the minimum?

Is it understandable to most people?

Does it promote cooperation and local self-reliance?

If you can answer "yes" to these questions, then the technology is an appropriate one to use.

It is difficult to pinpoint just when the term "appropriate technology" came into general usage. Perhaps it had its genesis on college campuses, in more advanced hippie communes, in the counter culture of the 1960s and '70s.

Rachel Carson had written about *The Sea Around Us*, and had followed with her best seller, *Silent Spring*. People—most notably students and teachers—talked about Carson's books and the problems brought on by indiscriminate chemical warfare against insects, weeds, and fungi. They, with Rachel Carson, sought more appropriate methods of control.

This author was not a warrior in the accepted sense. She was not an alarmist. She was a scientist who shunned publicity. However, she had discovered scientific facts too important not to be told. In death, she has become the patron saint of ecologists and environmentalists.

Rachel Carson laid the blame for the imminent poisoning of nature where it belonged—on mankind, one of the potential victims of his own folly. "Only within the moment of time represented by the present century has one species—man—acquired significant power to alter the nature of his world," she wrote in *Silent Spring*.

Rachel Carson started an environmental renaissance in America and part of Europe that has spread worldwide. The words "appropriate technology," coupled with "alternative energy," became familiar. Many other names followed: soft technology, organic technology, biotechnology. Some described it as "a new technology," and "people working together in new ways to suit the times."

When they met in the mid-'60s at the University of

Before the crowds come, Kate Janney sweeps up around the California Office of Appropriate Technology "New Possibilities Show." Note solar collector on rear of trailer for hot water demonstration.

Michigan at Ann Arbor, William W. McLarney and John H. Todd were doing research on fish behavior. Later, working together at San Diego State University, they discovered that fish which had ingested DDT became antisocial.

They became concerned that toxics that changed fish behavior might someday change human behavior as well. They decided to start a society to fight this omnipresent danger, and they called it the New Alchemy Institute. The name was inspired by a long-disused aim of ancient alchemy—to integrate science and the humanities.

In the early '70s, Todd and McLarney, with a few colleagues, founded the first New Alchemy center in the hills south of Cape Cod. From this point they spread the word of AT and began a number of experiments aimed at structuring a more self-reliant, ecology-minded sector in society.

If man could alter the nature of his world, as Rachel Carson had said, then he could alter it for the better, through AT methods and practices. So thought the people at the New Alchemy Institute.

They designed a smaller, high-yield method of gardening; they constructed "solar ponds" to provide a means for home owners and apartment dwellers to grow a large amount of edible fish; they built windmills, and solar ovens, and greenhouse hot-air collectors; they grew "agricultural forests" —densely planted fruit and nut trees grown as a source of high-nutritional foods. They disdained chemical insecticides, fungicides, and fertilizers.

The New Alchemy philosophy spread quickly. In less than a decade, it is known and taught throughout the world.

Meanwhile, London economist E. F. ("Fritz") Schumacher added a touch of hard-nosed business to the soft-technology picture without losing the sense of importance that people must take. In his book, *Small Is Beautiful,*

**Richard Wenn checks solar heater display in OAT trailer. Examples of energy alternatives are part of the "New Possibilities Show."**

Schumacher called for a time of reckoning, a closer look at the "capital assets" of mankind.

According to Schumacher, we have only looked at the "things we have produced" as capital: ". . . a large fund of scientific, technological, and other knowledge; an elaborate physical infrastructure; innumerable types of sophisticated capital equipment—" only a small part of the capital we are putting to everyday use.

Another part is there, overlooked: the elements that made the production possible—the natural capital.

Far larger is the capital provided by nature and not by man—and we don't even recognize it as such. This larger part is now being used up at an alarming rate, and that is why it is an absurd and suicidal error to believe, and act on that belief, that the problem of production has been solved.

Taking a close look at "natural assets" we must include the water, air, minerals, flora, and fauna as capital. Visualize this capital stored in a warehouse. Place that warehouse on a vehicle. Call that vehicle Spaceship Earth.

It is neither new nor original to call our planet a spaceship. Nor is it difficult to picture us riding on this spinning globe at thousands of miles per hour (as we see time) through a void toward no discernable terminal. There is no stopping this spaceship and getting off. No cargo ships head this way. Man is limited to what is at hand. When a resource is used up, there will be no replacement parts at a friendly way station.

Yet man takes what he wants from the warehouse, without thought of checking the supply manifest. He uses up reserves as though he need only put in a requisition to some high office for replenishment. He imprudently spends his nest egg as though it were a weekly paycheck to be duplicated every Saturday.

Fritz Schumacher believed that this is where man has erred most grievously: by actually liquidating his natural assets, man depends on nature to resupply what has been drawn from the First Natural Bank of Spaceship Earth—without having made a deposit. Through all his wasteful activities, man is deceiving himself. He is not independent at all!

Part of the limited natural assets man insists on squandering are labeled "fossil fuels." Under this heading are coal, crude oil, and natural gas. This asset had been laid by for hundreds of centuries, deep below the inner shell of the spaceship. Man found it easily accessible—perhaps by accident —when surface coal was discovered. Coal was mined in the colonies on a commercial basis in 1758, before the United States was even a nation. It is deposited throughout thirty-nine of the states and territories.

Often difficult and dangerous to extract from the warehouse, coal's value is undeniable. It is a source of heat and power. It can be converted into oils, gasoline, and such by-products as nylon textiles, imitation wood, foams. Even the aspirin tablet is a coal derivative.

The supply of coal in the natural bank is generous, but it is not inexhaustible, and an environmental tax must be levied on its extraction and processing. The tax is in pure air, blue skies, and the destruction of the land. Environmentalists say it is an important and precarious trade-off.

Petroleum—"rock oil"—has been known since antiquity. The Bible refers to "pitch" made from oil as an ingredient used to cement the walls of Babylon. Originally a medicinal or ointment, it has become industrially important only in relatively recent times.

Oil has flowed in many localities from natural springs. In 1859 Edwin L. Drake successfully drilled a well in northwestern Pennsylvania. It was 69 feet deep and produced fifteen barrels of oil a day. Soon low-octane fuels called "gasoline" were developed. The internal-combustion engine was invented; it ran on gasoline and was lubricated by refined oils and grease.

Other points of access to the natural oil warehouse were soon discovered: Texas, Oklahoma, California; Persia, Arabia, North Africa; Russia, Venezuela, the East Indies; all over the spaceship holes were drilled.

In 1980, the world's known conventional oil reserves totaled about 500 billion barrels. Soviet Russia had about 150 billion barrels, a little more than Saudi Arabia. Venezuela claimed to have "heavy oil" tar fields capable of producing another 500 billion barrels. Shale deposits in North America contained a few billion barrels more. Small deposits were discovered in the North Sea and in Indonesia.

But eagerly the industrial and automotive sector pounced upon each new discovery and expended the supply at a prodigious rate. It has been said that 60 percent of the world's oil was used by the United States, which has less than 6 percent of the world's population.

Within a period beginning with the end of World War II, the United States alone trebled its use of fossil-originated fuel and by-products, according to Schumacher during a 1972 symposium on "World Fuel in the Year 2000." That was a period of twenty-eight years. Projecting forward another twenty-eight years to 2000, Schumacher inquired: Would the United States again treble its usage? Then Schumacher, thinking farther into the future asked:

> What is so special about the year 2000? What about the year 2028, when the little children running about today will be planning for their retirement?

By the year 2028, wondered Fritz Schumacher, would there be another trebling? If so, would the inevitable end to fossil-fuel supply be reached?

The liquidation of these natural capital assets, Schumacher noted, had affected ". . . many worried men, right up to the White House . . . demanding ever more gigantic efforts to search for and exploit the remaining treasures of the world." Obviously man—particularly Western Man—was determined to draw the last of the natural assets before thinking of making any deposits into the First Natural Bank.

In his search for natural treasure man came upon uranium, which he discovered could be divided by nuclear fission under the most controlled circumstances, atom by split atom. The by-product gave the promise of being an unmatchable energy source.

Within a short time, a few problems arose: another by-product of atom fission was radioactive waste. It must be contained, transported, and stored in another part of the spaceship with extraordinary care.

Proponents and theorists in the nuclear camp said, "Don't worry about the waste. It's perfectly safe. It can be buried in salt mines, or in the desert; it can be shot to the sun in rockets; it can be glassified. We need the energy, and we need it now!"

Opponents said, "Wait just a minute! How do you know it's perfectly safe? Will you be around in a hundred years, or two, or three, or a thousand years to inspect the places where you propose to bury this deadly material?"

Then came Three Mile Island—and the debate flared anew. All of this debate is academic, according to those who espouse the Schumacher theory. Uranium, too, comes from the First Natural Bank. It is irreplaceable when used up. The world's stock of uranium, at last compilation, was in relatively short supply. The time had come for a reordering of priorities, while some assets still remained in the warehouse.


AT activists, following the common path of Rachel Carson, the New Alchemists, and E. F. Schumacher, are breaking a pioneer trail that private industry has suddenly recognized.

Theorists, having perfected their ideas, are ready to go into production. Design teams have plans drawn and ready themselves for a new eco-industrial period that makes the best use of all natural capital, without waste or pollution. New programs and projects are gaining acceptance.

However, an unusual deficiency has been noticed: the need for qualified men and women, oriented in AT theory, to put that theory into action. As AT spreads through the country, new career opportunities will develop. This book will help you to understand the attitude and approach that marks AT people. If this thinking appeals to you, you may be right for a career in these new fields.

In the early 1970s Sim Van der Ryn, a San Francisco architect, had become interested in urban habitat design, waste disposal, and new alternatives for conventional energy supply to heat and cool his buildings.

Van der Ryn had met with Edmund G. ("Jerry") Brown, Jr., when Brown was California secretary of state. It was an informal social gathering, held at the time Schumacher's book *Small Is Beautiful* was published. Brown found that he, Fritz Schumacher, and Sim Van der Ryn held a common philosophy.

Van der Ryn had learned of AT theory quite by chance —in his own kitchen. "I was preparing some vegetables," he says. "I was doing as I always did. I shoved the scraps into the garbage disposal and flushed them into the sewer system. It was quite natural."

A guest at mealtime who had been exposed to New Alchemy scolded Sim about his careless method of getting rid of vegetable waste. "Why don't you save the scraps?" Sim was asked. "Put them into a compost pile. Recycle them. It will be better for your flowers and shrubs than any fertilizer you can buy."

Thus began a new career in world stewardship. Sim Van der Ryn, for reasons we are sure even he may not understand, got "the message" that day in his kitchen.

When Jerry Brown was elected governor of California, he appointed Van der Ryn state architect. Remembering his talks with Brown, Van der Ryn wrote a preliminary paper that he presented to the governor's office. In the paper he proposed the concept of an Office of Appropriate Technology (OAT). The department was intended to furnish guidelines for future state architecture, but the role of OAT was quickly redefined.

This was perhaps the first time the term "appropriate technology" was brought into general use and the first time it attained governmental status at the state level.

On May 12, 1976, by executive order, Brown created OAT to assist both government and the people in a period of social transition, dealing with changing personal values, environmental stress, and diminishing resources. Four years later, OAT was recognized by the state legislature and was written into the statutes as a state agency, independent of the administrative offices.

After its founding, an official OAT statement said in part:

> The recognition that we live in a world of limited resources requires development of a conservative technology. As government tries to adapt to the new realities of diminishing resources and changing values, we must find ways . . . less wasteful, less costly and bureaucratic, less harmful to people and their environment . . .

To achieve these ends through the introduction of cost- and energy-saving alternatives, California OAT was charged with the responsibility to act as a catalyst for change in the areas of:


—job development
—resource conservation
—environmental protection
—community development.


OAT was originally financed through the Brown administration's Office of Planning and Research. Its funding—a mere $25,000 to begin with—was in direct proportion to its philosophy. To follow Sim Van der Ryn's list of priorities, the staff concentrated on waste and resource management; food production, including urban agriculture and farmers' markets; transportation and leisure, leaning heavily on alternative transit modes and bicycling, walking, and running; housing and domestic energy, particularly in retrofitting older buildings for solar applications; and industrial on-site energy alternatives.

For the past five years California OAT has grown, in a normal healthy way. It is now under control of the legislature, rather than the governor's office. While funding costs have risen to almost $1.25 million, savings attributed to OAT totaled over $13 million in fiscal year 1979–80. Some 42 people work under the OAT logo. Activities have multiplied. They include almost every energy project imaginable, such as small backyard solar alcohol stills, large biomass conversion, wind-energy systems, housing design, and toxic waste disposal.

Meanwhile, Richard Wenn and Kate Janney, with the

New Possibilities Show, carry abroad the OAT credo: Preserve the natural capital through conservation and AT.

One OAT spin-off has been Women in Energy, an organization formed by Janice Jacobson, OAT public information librarian, and some 70 professionals working in the field. "We have four task forces," says Jacobson. "We are interested in career development for women within the energy sector. We are involved with local action projects regarding energy. We have formed a state political action committee. And we have a networking program to contact other organizations, act as an outreach facility, and coordinate a job-referral service for women in energy."

Women in Energy concentrate more on conservation than resource choices; they are neither antinuclear nor pro-solar. However, they are women with faith in their work and are willing to put in time and effort outside their jobs to promote their strong beliefs.

AT is catching on rapidly in all sectors, public and private. "The markets for appropriate technology are varied and widely diffused," says the National Science Foundation, "but we include the small-scale farmer, the small-scale businessman, and the small-scale manufacturer, as well as large-scale activities."

In the following chapters you will find some of these activities—large scale and small—and meet some of the people involved. The AT door is opening wide. Please enter.

For You to Do Now:

Find technologies now in use within your immediate environment that might be considered inappropriate because they misuse irreplaceable natural capital assets. Try to find alternatives to serve their purpose. Take wood and metal shop courses in school that will help you learn to use hand tools.

JOB OPPORTUNITIES:

Working within appropriate technology runs the gamut from non-skilled labor to the highest degree of professionalism. Following each chapter there is a list of jobs available in that area. Some seventy separate career choices are included. *One is for you!*

# CHAPTER 2
# AT IN THE HOME



THE LIKLIK BUK
PAPUA NEW GUINEA, 1977

APPROPRIATE TECHNOLOGY, like charity, should begin at home.

It was 1973. The OPEC oil embargo had begun. Judy Dittmar and Ray Tretheway had met in Professor Richard Cooley's classes on environmental studies at the University of California, Santa Cruz, and enjoyed each other's company. Their shared environmental commitment and work in Santa Cruz recycling centers seemed compatible, and they married.

In 1974 Ray had an opportunity to do research in Washington, D. C., working with Robert Cahn on his book *Foot-*

*prints on the Planet*: *A Search for an Environmental Ethic.* The Tretheways stayed in Washington for three and one-half years, then decided to return to California for the birth of their first child, Elinore.

Sacramento is Ray's home town; Judy is from Seattle. A section of Sacramento called River Gardens, alongside a levee constructed in 1914 to reclaim land from the seasonal overflow of the American River, is a place of rich soil, a tiny enclave within the city limits with smaller older homes, vegetable gardens, and "country" feeling. It is only a few minutes by auto and not many more by bicycle from the state capital complex. Here the Tretheways decided to sink their roots.

Ray got a job with the state Department of Parks and Recreation. Judy did research on the environmentally designed home they would soon build; she spent a lot of time around the OAT library, furthering her knowledge of solar energy, heating with wood, insulation, and other AT applications.

One of the inaccurate claims about solar building is "it costs too much." The Tretheways built their completely solar home for $30,000 in 1979, when nonsolar homes of comparative size in the Sacramento market were priced from $60,000 to $80,000.

Inducements in solar architecture beyond environmental aspects are found in reduced utility costs. Annual cost of heating and cooling in the Tretheway home is extremely low. Their design—reached after many hours of library research and personal investigation—has given them a passive solar home that uses no gas or electricity except for cooking, lighting, and food refrigeration; much of their cooking is done in a solar oven. A small wood stove, fueled with forest gleanings, is adequate on cold winter nights.

Ray Tretheway admits that savings in construction costs were realized by his and Judy's combined efforts in putting the house together—with some timely help from friendly neighbors who assisted in raising the more difficult upper structure.

To share their solar-building experience the Tretheways began to open their home for inspection during local charity home tours. Soon Judy thought there might be a better way to spread their knowledge. Working with the Solar Syndicate, a small outlet for environmental odds and ends in Old Sacramento, she prepared a series of programs for anyone interested in alternative energy, conservation, gardening, and other self-reliant activities.

Offered in small classes, some at her home and some at on-site demonstrations, Judy's programs included lectures by solar architects, wind-power experts, engineers in solar hot-water heating, and technicians in window insulating and shading.

Programs for 1981 included landscaping for solar conservation, solar dehydrators, attached greenhouses, solar alcohol stills (backyard variety), and terratecture (below-ground dwellings). It is through such demonstrations and shared experiences that a new brand of American pioneer is blazing a path away from an almost total dependency on a single energy source: petroleum. A source that is obsolete, of prohibitive cost and environmental concern. It is a natural asset in danger of depletion.

No single area is more dependent on petroproducts than the American home. Space and water heat, cooking fuel, home furnishings, transportation (public and private), food and food packaging are all reliant in one form or another on petroenergy and petrochemicals. Petroleum dictates employment, governmental policy, and national economics. This

Workshop members learn about solar cooking on the patio of Ray and Judy Tretheway's passive solar home. Portable solar ovens heat up to over 350°, bake bread, cook all foods, with no energy cost.

condition, according to Fritz Schumacher, could be called efficient only ". . . if it obtained strikingly successful results in terms of human happiness, well-being, culture, peace and harmony."

That has not happened. It is a time for pioneering.

The energy source most favorable for exploitation is the sun; there is certainly no danger of depleting solar power. The only danger lies in the manner in which it is exploited.

Your plans for a career in this small world will be enhanced considerably if you hitch them to that not-too-distant star. In the near future, the sun will create more jobs and cause a resurgence in economic well-being never before realized upon this tiny spaceship.

Solar power encompasses direct energy, wind generation, biomass conversion, oceanthermal technology; it includes passive and active space heating, water heating, photovoltaic conversion. All of these facets of solar power offer exciting vistas for the entrepreneur of tomorrow. And all are available now for your study and eventual use.

The economy and employment in the twenty-first century will be based on alternative energy sources, as it was based on petroleum for the past eight decades. Now in the 1980s, the sun seems to be the likely alternative. So let us investigate solar power as it will relate to everyday living in our homes.

With the skyrocketing cost and doubtful availability of coal, oil, and electricity to heat and cool our homes, cook our food, heat our water, how do we cope? We turn to proven methods, some of them ancient, not popular in the modern sense until now, but definitely feasible.

## *PASSIVE (DIRECT THERMAL)*
## *HEATING AND COOLING*

Utilizes the direct rays of the sun to heat the air within buildings; hot air is circulated by convection; heat is stored on thermal walls and circulated naturally when the sun goes down. Cooling reverses the process: the thermal wall absorbs daytime heat and releases it at night. Thermal chimneys and underground "cool tubes" assist cold-air circulation.

## *ACTIVE (INDIRECT)*
## *HEATING AND COOLING*

Uses the sun to heat water and/or other substances usually on rooftop collectors. Gathered heat is transferred to hot-water tank for domestic use, for pumped circulation in heating system. Certain fluids that expand at moderately high temperatures are used to operate refrigeration units. Fans are used in active solar installations when necessary.

## *PHOTOVOLTAIC*
## *ELECTRICAL GENERATION*

Converts sunlight into direct current through specially designed silicon wafers; electricity can be used as produced or stored in batteries.

## *WIND GENERATION*

Windmills turn turbines that generate electric power.

## WOOD ENERGY

Wood burned in fireplaces and/or stoves heats interiors and domestic water.

## SOLAR GREENHOUSE

Sometimes called "walk-in heat collector," adds heat to building and provides warm space for growing food supplements.

## DISTILLATION

Turns vegetable waste (biomass) into alcohol for fuel.

## COMPOSTING

Sun turns vegetable waste into soil enricher.

The feasibility of solar heat was brought out as long ago as 1976 when a report prepared by the Mitre Corporation for the Energy Research and Development Administration (ERDA) said solar heat was already competitive with electricity in Atlanta; Bismarck, N. D.; Boston; Charleston, S. C.; Columbia, Mo.; Dallas; Grand Junction, Colo.; Los Angeles; Madison, Wis.; Miami; New York; and Washington, D. C.

Only Seattle, where hydroelectric power is cheap, showed an economic advantage for electric heating over solar. More recent studies will show that solar-generated energy is competitive with all other fuels, including natural gas, coal, and nuclear fission.

Your personal investigation of solar alternatives will lead directly to employment and, if you so choose, a rewarding career. Despite negative reactions among some who, through ignorance or blatant disregard of the facts, chide solar thinkers as flakes and dreamers, the sun appears to be the goal in home technology.

There is nothing new in relying on free solar heat for comfort and survival. The ancient Greeks placed their dwellings so the low winter sun warmed their living quarters. Two-story buildings were set to the north of single-story habitats, so as not to shade the lower structures. Courtyards divided buildings to allow slanting rays to reach all southern exposures. Wide overhanging roof extensions shaded interiors from overhead summer sun, aiding in modifying excessive heat.

The twelfth-century Anasazi Indians—the cliff dwellers we learned about in primary geography—faced their habitats southward. Taking advantage of natural caves in the mountainsides, they built adobe structures that soaked up heat during the day and released it at night. The natural cliff overhangs blocked off most of the intense high-angled summer sun.

For at least eight hundred years the peasants of northern China have built their homes in limestone bluffs, facing south. Not only are the interiors comfortably regulated in hot summers and cold winters; the tops of the houses are used for growing crops. Even some of their public buildings and schools are constructed in this fashion.

Modern Spanish laws forbid building a structure or planting a tree that will shade a neighbor's southern exposure. Similar laws are being passed throughout the United States and Europe.

Before the end of this century residences will have their major window spaces facing south, with overhangs to accomplish what cave openings did for the cliff dwellers. Solar collectors will heat water; photovoltaic cells will transmit electric power; more electricity will be wind generated. Conventional gas and electric sources will be used only as standby measures.

Redesigning older residences for appropriate technologies is not only feasible and practical—it is paying off in the job market. Federal, state, and local governments are gearing up training programs, and private foundations are making funds available to entrepreneurs willing to break technological barriers.

Retrofitting—as redesigning has been dubbed—is possible even in the most modest circumstances. This has been proven at the Farallones Institute's Integral Urban House in perhaps the drabbest section of Berkeley, California.

A group of environmental engineers, horticulturalists, and solar enthusiasts calling themselves the Farallones Institute purchased an old Victorian dwelling on the Berkeley flatlands in the industrial area. They transformed a hapless structure, doomed to the wrecker's ball, into an active demonstration of what people can do to improve the quality of their environment and their lives.

On a tiny city lot that surrounds the house, the institute included a vegetable garden employing minimal irrigation and cultivation techniques to provide a year-round supply of fresh food. In a corner near an alleyway, they built a round tank for raising fish. A hive supplies honey and bees for plant pollination.

Solar collectors for space heating and domestic water were installed. A homesite "gray water" system was designed to reclaim waste water for garden irrigation. A waterless biological toilet for converting human wastes into pathologically free soil amendment was built into the home. Facilities for raising rabbits and chickens were constructed, and dwarf fruit trees were strategically placed around the small yard. All walkways are of reclaimed wood chips, and the vegetable waste that does not feed the animals is composted in neat boxes along a fence line.

The dwelling houses two couples who make up part of the staff that utilizes the facilities as a teaching aid. The Integral Urban House staff offers its technical services to community groups, schools, and governmental agencies. They work with other organizations to develop programs in housing rehabilitation, community food raising, and neighborhood environmental educational projects.

The institute also assists individuals in developing energy- and resource-conserving techniques for their homes. Services range from designing solar heating systems to designing gardening and recycling systems. The staff works on a fee or contract basis.

Besides public tours, the Urban House staff offers a variety of short seminars and "hands-on" workshops on subjects relevant to self-reliance for the urban family. An internship program in Urban Whole Life Systems is offered on a quarterly basis to selected applicants. The program is designed to teach skills in food production, aquaculture, graywater cycling, composting, and alternative energy systems. Academic credit is available.

Similar workshops and internships are springing up around the country. Jobs and careers will be waiting for those alert enough to take advantage of these new programs. In the summer of 1980, according to national estimates, over 10,000 new jobs in appropriate technologies were opening up annually. This figure will grow rapidly as homes require alternatives to petroleum technology.

For You to Do Now:

Look about your home. How is it heated? How is the water heated? Is your home adequately insulated? Using your local library, do some research on home solar applications and retrofitting. Perhaps there are contractors doing this work in your neighborhood. Try to find a job in progress that you can visit. Take drafting and mechanical drawing courses in school.

Job Opportunities:

Teacher, architect, draftsman, engineer, landscape designer, gardener: all AT careers.

# CHAPTER 3
# AT IN THE COMMUNITY



As AT philosophy grows stronger in the home, it soon reaches out into the community. Projects such as New Village in Fayette County, western Pennsylvania, are born. Designed for an initial capacity of fifty families, New Village will expand to two hundred families within its first five years. Their goal: independence from public utilities through AT applications.

Literally a hands-on workshop, New Village residents have laid out their own streets and built their own homes. Housewives and mothers run bulldozers and finish cement;

coal miners become welders and pipe fitters. Theirs is a true community spirit.

The community cooperative idea is also strong in Milwaukee, Wisconsin, where a planned freeway was abandoned and replaced by a forty-block farmers' market and cooperative food-production center. Milwaukee's famous solid rye breads and pumpernickels, cheeses and sausages, and produce from neighboring community gardens are all sold at this Park West Cooperative.

Pittsburgh, Chicago, Syracuse, Philadelphia—cities across the country have started "whole life systems" community undertakings. It has rightfully been called "the green revolution." Neighborhood groups and national resource people under such colorful names as Green Guerrillas, Center for Neighborhood Technology, Institute for Local Self-Reliance, Trust for Public Lands, and South Bronx People's Development Corporation are proliferating.

Nowhere is the feeling of community more strong than in a neighborhood gardening project. These are the town halls of the green revolution. "Neighborhoods that have community gardens generally coalesce around the garden," says Rosemary Menninger, California's State Community Garden coordinator. "It becomes a meeting place."

Emphasizing that urbanization often diminishes community spirit, Menninger says, "The garden brings together people who have never worked together. It has a positive effect on the surroundings and gives people a sense of power." According to her, community gardens offer alternatives to young people as well as adults. Truancy is reduced and vandalism problems are eliminated as young people learn to share and respect the property of others. Neighborhood pride is enhanced in a positive manner.

Menninger's duties include convincing bureaucratic

state agencies to make available nonspecified funds, land, and materials for civic garden projects. "For example," she explains, "according to law a portion of money raised through the California personalized license plate fund could be used for school gardens."

Rosemary Menninger is practiced in bureaucratic survival. One of her first jobs after college was to write fund-raising programs for the Navajo Indians in Arizona. Living frugally in trading-post settlements in the Four Corners area near Canyon de Chelly, she was successful in presenting a proposal that brought the Navajos a $6 million congressional grant. At the same time, working with a medicine man and translated tape recordings, she wrote textbooks on Navajo history.

**Vicki Masterson demonstrates the craft of weaving to entranced students.**

While with the Navajos she saw "people growing food in places where it was thought impossible to grow food." She saw corn flourishing in dry desert washes, watered in the spring by freshets and later, in the 100-plus heat of summer, by hand-carried containers.

This experience piqued her interest in gardening under adverse conditions. Later, while working as a drug-treatment center secretary in San Francisco, where good topsoil is meager, that interest was enforced when she attended a Bay area organic farming conference. There she met Huey Johnson, California secretary of resources, who at that time worked for the Nature Conservancy.

Through Huey Johnson, Menninger received a grant to found the Institute of Applied Ecology (IAE). This group created the highly successful San Francisco Community Garden Program. On city land, leased for a dollar a year, a composting program was begun (compost is a must in San Francisco); a garden worked by teen-age delinquent girls soon thrived on the now-fertile ground. Using institutional land as an untapped resource, IAE initiated gardens on hospital, youth guidance, and senior citizen properties, and on vacant lots.

"We even started one with General Motors at their Fremont assembly plant," says Menninger. "That includes over a hundred gardeners and their families." Eventually Menninger met in conference with state officials, Gov. Jerry Brown among them. "I asked what resources they had in their agencies that would apply to community gardening," she recalls.

The Department of Food and Agriculture, she discovered, was researching plant propagation with home gardeners in mind. General Services had surplus equipment available. The Bureau of Outdoor Recreation had held conferences to

In the midst of evolving technologies, Kate Janney waters her herb garden. A mural showing the San Francisco Community Garden adds dimension.

promote gardening as a means of recreation. Other agencies offered diverse resources.

Rosemary Menninger undertook the responsibility of bringing all these agencies and their resources together. "Today there are more than a thousand community gardens in California," she attests, "and over one hundred and twenty community programs. My goal is to make gardens available to everyone, of all ages, and in every economic condition."

Paolo Soleri is a small man with a giant, slowly evolving dream. With the singleness of purpose that emulates an ant striving to move a boulder, Soleri—architect, artist, and aesthete—together with a kaleidoscopic mix of volunteers, is building a unique town called Arcosanti in the Arizona desert. Arcosanti is carved out of south-facing sandstone cliffs far from utility lines and civic amenities.

Soleri calls this architectural carving of niches in stark canyon and arroyo walls "arcology." The term is derived from *arcosolium*—the recessed places in Roman catacombs used for interment of Christian martyrs, as well as other enemies of the political realm. Modeled on the Anasazi Indian principle of solar heat and passive cooling, Arcosanti will someday be—if Soleri's dream comes true—a self-sufficient habitat, a jumble of apartments, work spaces, and bazaars where transit is unnecessary and all community affairs interrelate.

A nonprofit group called the Arcology Circle, based on some of Paolo Soleri's ideas, thought that such interesting theories should not be used solely in the Arizona badlands and sought out an urban neighborhood where at least the rudiments of the dream could be spread. They were drawn to Berkeley, California, where they hired David Musnick, of the Farallones Integral Urban House staff, to coordinate an Integral Neighborhood project. Quoting a West Berkeley Project report:

An integral neighborhood is one in which all systems—social, economic, architectural, technical, biological, and ecological are integral to one another; in which wastes become resources, energy is conserved, cooperative effort results in economic advantage to the neighbors; transportation-related problems such as wasted time in commuting, massive energy consumption, air pollution, and hazard to life are largely solved at the level of causes by building so that living, working, and learning are in close proximity with one another.

Pointing out that many New Town and conventional urban renewal projects have failed, Integral Neighborhood people blame the lack of an "ecosystems" approach to the planning process and the failure to include local residents in the design and development of planned neighborhood systems.

We believe Integral Neighborhoods to be a solution to many of the social and environmental problems of our cities. They are part of the process of human ecological evolution as well.

As the ecosystems experiment continued through the efforts of the Farallones Institute, the New Alchemists, and Integral Urban House and Neighborhoods' staffs, it became obvious that there was a need for another adjunct to the community teaching-learning process. In 1975, the Farallones Rural Center was established. Some 60 miles north of San Francisco, nestled into Sonoma County hills, the rural center offers a setting for appropriate technologies to be practiced in an everyday environment.

Sim Van der Ryn, president of the Farallones board of directors, said in December, 1977:

A primary objective of our education program should be to provide training in appropriate technology to people who have active roles in government, community groups, public and private institutions.

We should focus on extending our prototypes to existing urban neighborhoods and rural areas, as well as work to design new ecotopian communities built with private or public capital. The vision of a biologically stable solar city which derives its energy from the sun, recycles its own wastes without pollution, and grows its own food, can be realized now.

We need to extend the basis for our own economic self-sufficiency through development of a productive agricultural project which demonstrates competitive small scale farming practices and trains new agriculturalists.

We must expand our professional staff and market its expertise in the design of integrated whole systems.

Van der Ryn pointed out that this vision will not be easily implemented. The Western world of limited resources is often greedy and apathetic, he feels. People try desperately to "use up all they can now, without thought for a future."

We have come no longer to expect wisdom or leadership from our politicians, whose vision seldom extends beyond the next election.

So what is needed, Van der Ryn believes, is to help others choose a way for themselves. To keep the visions alive. Make them real. And then let the world do the work in its own way.

The community learning place selected by the Farallones Institute is idyllic. Situated deep in the Coast Range, just west of the tiny town of Occidental about 8 miles from the Pacific Ocean, the rural center takes up some 80 acres, part of it wooded, with a sunwashed area for garden space in the center.

Around one side of the cleared space are a dozen structures: a small office with a library, a blacksmith shop, woodworking and welding shops, classrooms, solar cabins and

A view of the Farallones Rural Center administration buildings
as seen from the barn on a nearby hill.

**Farallones Rural Center cabins are warmed by solar hot air collectors and wood stoves. Note dwarf fruit orchard in foreground behind wheelbarrow.**

solar greenhouses, a community solar shower room, a community kitchen with dining room. (In fine weather, most meals are eaten outside in the meadow area.) Across a narrow roadway on the side of a hill stands a big timber-frame barn.

All of the buildings were erected by hands-on classes in all the skills necessary to create the center: carpentry, woodworking, plumbing, tile making, and ironmongering. Each took an important part in the process. A core group of staff members worked side by side with students and apprentices to develop the community. What evolved is a successful, dynamic educational organization.

The community varies in population, averaging about sixteen members living on-site. Periodic workshops may add as many as twenty-five, although the center becomes crowded with that many. Summer finds most students camping out, as housing is limited. Peace Corps volunteers are numbered among the center students; it was they who constructed several of the experimental solar cabins.

Weekend workshops—twelve to twenty participants—learn environmental horticulture, biological soil fertility, blacksmithing, and such how-tos as breadbox solar water heaters and solar food dehydrators. Fees range from $45 to $75 per weekend course, including room and board.

Although appropriate technology philosophy is taught throughout the curricula, a separate course on AT is featured each year, with such distinguished guest teachers as Tom Bender, editor of *RAIN* magazine, and Ken Darrow, editor of *Appropriate Technology Sourcebook*.

The center emphasizes the desperate need for practical skills and has been concerned with creating a community of people who can live from the produce of their own hands, eat their own vegetables, recycle their own wastes, and become self-sufficient within their own community.

To provide a "cottage industry" for the center, a ceramics shop prospers under the direction of Ben Katz. A blacksmith shop is under the careful eye and strong hands of Andrew Atkeison. Ceramist Katz produces tableware and bricks, floor tile, and novelties. Atkeison makes greenhouse hardware, latches, gates, and tools and a fine line of wrought iron special design accessories.

The center gardening instructor is Robert Kourick, a landscape architect who specializes in "edible landscapes." A successful landscaper in Marin County, he is developing methods of growing ornamental plants along with the edible varieties for maximum beauty, minimum upkeep, and perennial food yields. He uses plants for pest and erosion control and for phosphorous fertilizer production.

The profusion of growing things, even in winter, attests to Kourick's methods and assistant Charles Little's care.

There is adequate produce to export to urban markets, and the sale of cut flowers is a source of income for the Rural Center.

Kourick is also responsible for planting a new type of genetic dwarf fruit tree—Bing cherry, peach, nectarine, almond—within the center garden area. These trees, only recently developed by Floyd Zaiger of Modesto, California, grow to a height of 6 feet and can be planted as close together as 18 inches, or even closer, to achieve an "edible hedge" in the case of the Bing cherry. The fruit is normal size, the trees need not be pruned, and such annual problems as leaf curl are virtually nonexistent.

This strain of dwarf trees could well be the answer for communities seeking fresh fruit for canning or dehydrating in locales where land is at a premium. They grow slowly, reaching maturity late, and will live for twenty years or more in half-barrel-size containers on apartment terraces or fire escapes.

The Farallones Rural Center, as well as the Integral Urban House, has attracted much attention in the media during its short lifetime. Such national publications as *Smithsonian, The Atlantic Monthly, Hudson Homes, Rotarian, New West, Sunset,* and *Mother Earth News* have all featured Farallones' activities. "In sum, our publicity efforts are moving in a positive direction," says Ted Barnes, institute media coordinator. "The news media to date has been generous with a positive attitude toward us and so long as we continue to generate new approaches to ecological problem solving, we will no doubt continue to get our word out through news stories. Public response is also positive, but we must take care not to alienate our audience with exaggerated claims or sensationalism. The Farallones Institute embodies the overlapping value systems of consumerism, environ-

Seeds for Farallones Rural Center spring gardens are sprouted in solar greenhouse, which also acts as major heat collector for adjoining building.

Charles Little, rural center gardener, tends his early spring vegetables. Covers protect bedding plants from night frosts.

mentalism and appropriate technology, and our use of media must be conducted in a manner reflecting our integrity."

At the time the Farallones Institute was starting its Urban House and Rural Center, 400 miles south another community activity completely unrelated had begun to unfold. Valerie Pope, director of the San Bernardino West Side Community Development Corporation, was faced with a dilemma. Of 670 homes in her community, approximately 400 were vacant. "Boarded up. Weeds growing. Vandalized. Gutted out. Burnt." That's the way she describes conditions in this primarily black neighborhood.

"Houses had been sitting unoccupied for from five to seven years," she says. The banks and lending agencies had "red-lined" the community, and money for improvements was nonexistent. In some cases, the houses had been turned back to the Veterans Administration, which had guaranteed mortgages. As a whole, the West Side Community seemed doomed.

"We were on kind of a treadmill," Valerie Pope told us. "In many cases some of our parents were on welfare. And our kids were on welfare. The schools had been remiss in preparing our young people for employment. So we felt we had to come up with some solutions to our problems."

In search of some "attention catcher" to use as leverage for procuring funds to rehabilitate the neighborhood, Pope—who also was county chairperson of the Welfare Rights Organization—conferred with people experienced with Housing and Urban Development (HUD) officials. They knew that welfare, low-income, and elderly families have difficulty in keeping up with soaring costs, particularly that of natural gas for heating. It was decided that solar was the direction to take.

Calling on the expertise of semiretired engineer Nate Rekosh for technical advice, and showing a willingness to start small, the West Side CDC presented a plan to HUD that could be used not only in the San Bernardino community, but in other run-down neighborhoods across the country, as well as in new developments.

They began with a grant for $5,000 that allowed them to open an office in a spare room behind the neighborhood post office. Initial outlines led to a $25,000 grant. Then came Comprehensive Employment Training Act (CETA) money. The CDC basic plan was simple in theory, but quite complex to install: beginning with a group of ten houses on two blocks with contiguous back-lot boundaries, the plan called for a bank of solar collectors through which water would be heated and delivered to an underground tank reservoir from which all the homes could draw.

The tank, a huge 5,500-gallon size, was insulated with polyurethane, acrylic paint, and a plastic blanket. It was buried in a deep hole in a central area between houses. Settled on a 5-ton concrete slab, reinforced with steel, the earthquakeproof tank was made large enough to supply five more houses should neighbors decide they too would like to tie into the system.

Sufficient heat was conveyed to the houses to heat the air and supply hot water for all uses. Seldom was the conventional gas-heat supply required as a backup, even during the coldest, cloudiest winter days and nights. Enough heat was stored within the tank to last for a considerable span of sunless days. "Ours was a very visible program," Pope says. "We had open house eight hours a day. People get turned on to solar when they see it installed and at work."

However, this successful application of appropriate technology is only part of the story. As activity grew around the small CDC office, it was necessary to seek larger quarters. They moved to an abandoned shopping center that had been a meeting place for roving bands of aimless young members of the community. The CDC office became an awareness center where people shared experiences, got career counseling, held rap sessions. Communications were opened to city hall and the police department; CDC members formed a "crime fighters" hot line. Gradually new businesses were attracted to the once-forlorn shopping center. It is now a thriving business center within the community.

To accomplish this it was necessary to begin a training program for unemployed, inexperienced young people from the community. But before the trainees could begin to learn skills, it was mandatory to show the importance of coming to work on time every day, accepting instructions, performing whatever jobs were required by an employer. "We began with twenty-five trainees in the program," Valerie Pope remembers. "Young people with no marketable skills or work experience. I can tell you that very few of them knew how to work. We were concerned with them coming out of the program with good skills, not going out on minimum-wage jobs. We place them with companies that can offer some security for stable employment."

Men and women of all races and backgrounds learned not only about solar applications, but construction in general. Carpentry, plumbing, electrical wiring, cement work, roofing—all marketable skills. Secretarial training was included. The trainees and CDC staff did all the work on the solar installation and rehabilitation. "We were all learning, believe me," Valerie Pope laughs.

Along with the initial rehabilitation of the ten solar

homes, a companion program was begun. Repair work was offered to those whose homes were on the verge of dilapidation. Lawns were renovated and kept trim. Roofs and wiring and plumbing were put into good working order. There was no cost for this service for elderly citizens and a minimal charge was made to those of low income.

All the homes in the San Bernardino West Side community have not been rehabilitated. But they have made a good beginning. As people seek community support, and become self-sustaining in their energy requirements through community efforts, the cities will become less a place for decay and vandalism, and more a place for renewed viability.

FOR YOU TO DO NOW:

Find a community-oriented program such as gardening, solar technology, recycling, or building rehabilitation within your own town or community to work with. If none is available, try to start one with your friends and families. Get them involved. Start your own home garden, no matter how small. Learn all you can about the soil, growing conditions, and good vegetables to grow in your area. Take electrical shop, electrical wiring, diagraming, and theory classes in school.

JOB OPPORTUNITIES:

Social worker, community case-worker, horticulturist, blacksmith, artist, writer, secretary, cook: more AT careers.

# CHAPTER 4
# AT IN THE BIG APPLE AND OTHER CITIES

*THERE IS NOTHING WRONG IN ASKING FOR HELP WHEN YOU REALLY NEED IT, THE PROBLEM IS THAT SOME KINDS OF HELP LOCK US INTO PERMANENT ONGOING DEPENDENCY UPON HELP*

THE LIKLIK BUK
PAPUA NEW GUINEA, 1977

APPROPRIATE TECHNOLOGY as practiced in the sylvan Farallones Institute Rural Center, or in a low-income community in suburban San Bernardino, would seem far removed from its counterpart found in New York City. But a brief look into natural assets, resources, and physical needs in the Big Apple (as New York is colloquially called) shows similarities between the two coastal areas.

The Energy Task Force (ETF) is a group of designers, builders, and educators that advises low-income, grass-roots organizations in New York City on energy-related matters.

Adopt-a-Building is a nonprofit interfaith agency that works on the Lower East Side of Manhattan to develop and reclaim decent low-income housing. Working in a loosely knit relationship, the two groups combine "sweat equity" building, conservation, commercial revitalization, open-space development, and community planning in an effort to save what remains of the older ghetto neighborhoods.

We met with Margaret Morgan, executive director of ETF, and Linda Cohen, Adopt-a-Building community planner, and heard them air their dreams and frustrations. It was apparent that both young women shared the same goals as members of California OAT, Farallones Institute founders, and AT people everywhere: conserve natural assets while creating a viable, peaceful environment for everyone.

"Here in *Loisaida*—that, by the way, is a Spanish derivation for *Lower East Side of* New York City—we have a fourteen-block area of century-old tenements in various conditions of decay," says Linda Cohen. She is dark-haired and vivacious and was educated at Goddard College, Vermont.

Margaret Morgan, slim, energetic, artistic, with a B.A. from Bennington and two M.A.'s, from Columbia and the New School for Social Research, is equally dedicated. She states their case well. "Groups like Adopt-a-Building are a response to what has been going on in New York. Landlords were able to maintain buildings at a reasonable level where people could live in them and they could get their rent money. Then, as maintenance and energy costs rose, it became less profitable. So a whole series of landlords systematically burned buildings and abandoned them. Often they collect insurance, buy new properties, and begin the whole process over again."

Adopt-a-Building leaders, finding many of the abandoned buildings structurally sound, hit upon a plan to purchase some of them from among the twelve thousand properties owned by the city of New York. "Government interest has been to knock them down, get the bulldozers in there, and rebuild," says Linda Cohen. "We thought that the structurally sound buildings that were left in our communities could be rehabilitated at lower cost than any new construction project."

They called on tenants still living in abandoned shells of buildings to join in the struggle to survive. In Loisaida, when we spoke with Cohen and Morgan in the spring of 1980, 30 percent of the buildings still occupied were deteriorating so quickly that soon they too would follow the same pattern. The area resembles a war scene—piles of rubble; one in five buildings abandoned; one in ten is now an empty lot where buildings once stood, representing one-third of the community's living space, lost to its people. As you read this, the loss will be far greater. It is devastating.

Linda Cohen refers to poor boiler maintenance as a leading cause for building decline. When the boilers cease to function, the buildings soon follow the abandonment trend. Icy apartments are not conducive to happy tenants. But there are few other places for the tenants to go. In a year-after-year battle to save the neighborhoods, often it seems to Cohen that the fight is a losing one. "It's been really hard," she says. "A lot has been against us. Whenever a new program comes up, the money's there, but it is never spent. Seed money is turned back to the federal government and spent on other programs."

Adopt-a-Building persevered and enlisted community residents in their revitalization plan. As the organization effort began, the tenants were timid. But they joined in rent strikes—"No Heat, No Rent"—saved their rent money, pooled it, and were finally able to buy their buildings. People used to living as renters were afraid at first even to begin knocking down walls for renovating. But that was the plan, to rehabilitate these old shells with their own effort and sweat. (Hence the term "sweat equity.") The work united the community. Soon a feeling of pride prevailed. They found a sense of need, of self-worth.

"You have a much stronger sense of accomplishment," says Emma Azeveda, an erstwhile tenant at 55 Avenue C, who had worked to rehab their building. "More than if your landlord did it for you. It would be nice to sit back and have people do things for you. But there's an entirely different feeling when you do it yourself."

Working with city government, Adopt-a-Building earned the right to determine which buildings could be saved. Their engineering staff checks the buildings separately. "A certain number of structures are not sound and need to come down," Linda Cohen asserts. "The ones that get our okay are saved. Then the city is supposed to sell the buildings to the tenants for $250 per unit. That's from ten to twenty-five or thirty units per building, six-story tenements." She hesitates. "But the city's programs change so quickly, and they change their guidelines so quickly that it becomes almost impossible to actually get these buildings and have the tenants take ownership."

In cases where buildings are razed they try to fit in another kind of land use, such as a playground or park, or a community garden. Block associations are able to purchase vacant lots through the Trust for Public Land, another agency; the price is usually around $500.

Energy Task Force enters the picture when rehabilitation begins. "Burned-out buildings—what we call 'gut rehab' —are ideal for energy-conservation work," insists Margaret Morgan. Then an educational program starts. "For some reason, people don't want to hear about conservation," says a puzzled Morgan. "Their notion is that somehow they are going to deny themselves something."

Just the opposite happens, according to Morgan. Buildings in New York are often drafty. Windows and doors leak heat. Oversized boilers, when they work, tend to overheat apartments. Windows are wide open in the middle of winter because it is so hot inside. Drafts rush toward the openings. And New York cannot afford to waste the fuel.

"If you're going to do a gut rehab of this kind, you can insulate the buildings," says Morgan, "cut down on the drafts. When we do an energy rehab, we disconnect the radiators. Many of them are never reconnected, because just closing off the drafts is sufficient to keep rooms warm."

Margaret Morgan's eyes become animated as she describes a gut rehab. "We drop the ceiling on top floors to insulate the roof. We actually do this while people are living in the apartments. We insulate the walls, make stud walls where necessary. We tighten the windows and rehang doors. We put thermal shutters on the windows. We repair the boilers, fix flu systems where fireplaces are working, put flow restriction valves on water pipes. All these are simple techniques. But," she adds thoughtfully, "the trouble is that no one does them."

Morgan decries the architects and engineers who will do a rehabilitation for $200,000 and not put in the $7,000 necessary to complete a conservation rehab. The buildings remain drafty and poorly heated. "We did an energy audit for a building at 219 East Fourth Street," she recalls. "From our estimates, the people got a $12,000 grant. With ten units in the building we figured we'd invest $1,000 per unit. Through an energy-conservation rehab, we reduced the fuel bills by 37 percent. People living in the building can't get over the fact that there were no more drafts, that it is so livable."

ETF pushes solar energy. "But we can't even think about solar energy unless we start with energy conservation," Morgan says. "The vision people have when they think about solar is a solar home in New Mexico or California. Our vision is different. When we think solar, we think of collectors on tenement rooftops and windmills taking advantage of Lower East Side breezes."

One of the first buildings renovated by a sweat-equity group led by Adopt-a-Building was at 519 Eleventh Street. ETF talked to the people involved with the rehab and convinced them that if they were serious about long-term ownership, not short-term investment, they should think in terms of conservation and solar. New York's first "modern" windmill was installed on the Eleventh Street rooftop. Actually, it is an old second-hand mill, but it is the first since the Dutch settlers made squeaking wooden models commonplace along New York riverfronts. Consolidated Edison, the local power company, can easily view the windtower from its offices. The windmill is capable of generating enough electricity to shunt some back to the Con Ed grid, turning the tenants' meters backward.

"The horror of that arrangement," Morgan laughs ruefully, "is that we pay the regular price of ten cents per kilowatt hour for electricity we use, but according to the tariff agreement, residents at 519 only get two cents per kilowatt for what their mill generates. Furthermore, they charge them for the equipment necessary to monitor the amount of electricity the residents sell them."

Wind currents that pass over the Eleventh Street roof are not great enough to generate sufficient power to meet all electrical needs in the building. However, the full value of wind power can be attested to by Bronx Frontier, another technical assistance group with whom ETF is associated. Their Hunts Point site is an excellent place for their windmill, a large commercial-type 40-kw generator that supplies electrical needs for aerating compost gathered from the huge produce market situated in this port area. The vegetable waste compost is in turn distributed to urban gardeners for use as soil amendments.

ETF's work goes further than the actual tasks that keep them busy in the rehab field. Training solar installers is their latest, and potentially most productive, project. "We trained fifteen people through CETA during 1979 and 1980," proclaims Margaret Morgan proudly. "We got a grant to do twelve systems around the city, on all kinds of housing stock. The idea is to show that solar is not just a safe energy alternative, but a way of bringing jobs to low-income neighborhoods."

The CETA workers installed solar units in six low-income single-family dwellings and six multifamily buildings under ETF supervision. There were two women on the first crew. ETF hopes for a great deal more work in the next decade. "We also have trained people from the South Bronx, Harlem, and Brooklyn, as well as from the Lower East Side, to become community energy auditors," Morgan says. "They determine the condition of buildings, how to make them energy efficient. However, after we got them trained, it was hard to get anyone interested in the service. What we'd like to do is link them up with an energy retrofit service. We could start with windows, for instance. We have crews trained to repair and replace windows. It's unglamorous work, but it is highly necessary."

Another conservation facet emerged when, without project money to proceed in a retrofit service, ETF went into the boiler cleaning, repair, and maintenance business. "I taught that class," Margaret Morgan says gleefully. It is hard to believe when one notices her tapered, artistic fingers. "The landlords never cleaned the boilers," she continues. "Some boilers haven't been cleaned for ten years. Every quarter inch of soot and scale reduces the efficiency of a boiler. A regular inspection of every boiler in the city and a subsequent cleaning—a pretty minor activity—could reduce fuel bills by fifteen percent."

Jimmy Breslin, nationally syndicated columnist, in a story published several years ago, brought up a fact of slumlord life when he wrote about tax shelters in housing rehabilitation, specifically among New York tenements and projects. Investors, wrote Breslin, through famous brokerage houses put up minimal amounts of capital and end up with tax write-offs totaling as high as a quarter of a million dollars. These landlords, according to Breslin, are usually absentees, living in far-off locales—Ohio, or Beverly Hills, or the Middle East. ". . . 80 percent of the people investing in New York projects are from out of town," wrote Breslin. They never see their property. And they never see their tenants, either. They have little interest in their tenants well-being.

"Where do all the people go when they must leave these abandoned New York buildings?" we asked Margaret Morgan. "That's interesting," she answered thoughtfully. "No one ever asks that question in New York. The truth lies in the gentrification plans, through which the developers hope to reverse the tides of rich people moving out into the suburbs. Now they are trying to move the rich people back into the city and the poor people out into the suburbs. That's essentially what's happening. However, it hasn't been formalized." She laughs grimly. "There are no shuttle services."

Despite their frustrations with government bureaucracy,

both women hold a strong view of a better tomorrow. "We must get people to take an interest in developing neighborhoods for the people who live here," Linda Cohen believes. "It is happening in many cities across the country where old neighborhoods are close to business districts, and energy costs rise; suburbia moves back to the city. The gentrification process has begun. People are being displaced. We can't lose the people who have been committed to raising community standards."

Margaret Morgan, speaking for Energy Task Force, says, "Our goal is to take people who have learned basic skills through this housing movement and use those skills in energy conservation and solar energy work. Because all over the country people have done studies that say the place for jobs in the next ten years will be in solar energy and energy conservation. We have been trying to make sure that those jobs go to low-income people for work that's needed in the community, to maintain the integrity of the community, rather than for the gentrification that is taking place."

Our visit ends as Margaret Morgan muses: "The question is—does the sun set or rise on New York City?"

AT community activities have influenced some, if not many, of America's cities. San Diego, California, officials have passed an ordinance that requires use of solar energy for water heating in all new residential construction. In Narragansett, Rhode Island, AT activists have built a $21,000 solar-powered public bathroom.

The city of Winooski, Vermont, led by the 100-member Golden Onion Dome Club, is considering the possibility of covering the entire city with a solar air-conditioned geodesic dome.

Las Vegas, Nevada, will soon have twenty-five solar-powered geodesic domes and solar collectors for their "desert animals of the world" showcase zoo. One dome houses a bat exhibit in a cavelike environment. Other domes offer sun shelters for visitors; from inside they can observe the bighorn sheep, coyotes, reptiles, ostriches, and other desert animals that thrive in the hot, dry Nevada climate outside. Restaurants and offices are all under solar air-conditioned domes.

Cities from the Eastern Seaboard to the West Coast are studying building codes and proposing regulations to save energy and improve the environment. However, none come close to the city of Davis, California.

President Carter, in February, 1980, pointed to Davis as having found the solution to energy problems by cutting its total use by 35 percent. "The citizens of Davis have done a tremendous job," he told the convening National Association of Counties. Through following standards set by Davis, Carter said, ". . . we are better able to understand ourselves and to understand the tough choices that Americans must make in facing the challenges of the future."

The Davis decision was not made easily. The city is a university town of some 37,000, situated 15 miles from the state capital, Sacramento. It became "Aggie Town" in 1911, when the California State Agricultural College was founded. It drew its student body from the farms that dot the rich Sacramento and San Joaquin river valleys; a few came from the San Francisco Bay area and from Los Angeles.

Davis made no pretense of greatness in those days and contentedly went about the business of genetic biology and animal husbandry. After World War II, the University of California began to bulge at its respective seams on the Berkeley and Los Angeles campuses. Soon Davis became a burgeoning, full-fledged university campus in its own right; their medical, law, and other professional schools drew students from around the world. It found itself with high-rise dormitories, housing problems, and big-city traffic snarls.

But Davis went to work on its difficulties through environmental planning and has become a model for the rest of the country if not the world. It became a front-runner in a national movement to prioritize housing on a municipal plan without calling in state or federal agencies to set guidelines.

Some of the Davis plan could be put into practice by almost any city in the nation. All of the Davis philosophy could be implemented universally.

The following is part of what has been going on in Davis:

- Bicycles are a major mode of transportation. Downtown traffic is 40 percent bicycles; 90 percent of the riders are adults.
- Bicycle paths were constructed in new subdivisions; storage lockers for bicycles can be found around town; bike-lane lines were drawn on all major streets.
- Solar power is used for heating and cooling in two thousand homes. New subdivisions rely solely on solar, with wood stove backups and natural gas for emergency use.
- Trash collections are segregated: garbage in one load, recyclables—cans, glass, aluminum—in another.
- Low- and moderate-income housing is included in all new housing allocations.
- Housing-unit rentals are provided for in a variety of sizes and costs.
- Prime agricultural lands—"a limited resource of significant statewide importance"—that surround Davis are protected by strict zoning ordinances.
- Green spaces, parks, south-oriented buildings, complete insulation, and a nonspeculation rule for home-buyers are all part of the Davis Housing Ordinance.

That the Davis plan works is undeniable. In addition to the energy-consumption cut of 35 percent, gasoline usage has been reduced by 25 percent; per capita electric power, by nearly one-fifth; natural gas, by 30 percent. The feeling of pride is extremely high for any city, and remarkable in a college town where friction often rises between campus and "townies."

Even the developers and builders seem happy. At first the stringent codes left them grumbling, and several left the area vowing never to return. But some of the more creative sensed an opportunity not only to conform but to improve on the ordinances with new ideas in architecture and art.

One of these is Michael Corbett, who has been called by Parisian writers the "master of bioclimatic architecture." Corbett takes this accolade in stride. "I didn't even give solar, or energy, or the type of home we are building today a passing thought ten years ago," he says. Corbett admits his first houses were monsters that consumed great amounts of energy. But by the fall of 1980, his introductory environmental project, Village Homes, had been completed. Village Homes is a passive solar development of 217 dwellings on 70 acres near Davis's western city limits.

All Village Homes face the sun. Each has a passive system that heats and cools without benefit of other power. Some houses are earth-covered sod structures (owners call them "soddies"). Some use walk-in heat collectors (greenhouses). All are clustered around greenbelts, and bike trails meander between them. Streets are narrow to save asphalt and to lessen heat reflection in summer. Individual privacy is assured by landscaping and courtyards. Residents grow vegetables without inhibition, often substituting corn for front-yard lawns. People seem to enjoy living in the Village

Home environment: in the years since its inception, fewer than half a dozen families have moved.

Nationwide, all levels of government—city, state, and federal—are being asked to pay some heed to the squandering of resources in cities. "There are no perfect solutions," says

**Homes in a "Solar Village," Davis, California. Vegetable gardens replace lawns, and bike trails meander throughout neighborhoods. Note windows shaded by overhanging eaves and solar hot-water collectors on each roof.**

Gloria Shepard McGregor, community development director for the city of Davis. "Explorations of all kinds have their moments of glory and moments of pain—but that's what the evolvement and growth of humanities—and cities—is all about."

Nonetheless, the world watches. According to Richard ("Rick") Stone, DOE's director of the office of intergovernmental affairs, there is international interest in the Davis program, although foreigners do not always get the name right. "I talk to Japanese industrialists," Stone says. "They all say, 'Tell us about Davisville.' And Germans come over. 'What are they doing now in Davidville?' they ask. People from all over are talking about what you have done in Davis, even if they have trouble with the name. But now you have another job to do. You have to sell Davis to the rest of the nation."

That, of course, is the commitment of all AT people: To sell—with prudence—AT ideology.

### For You to Do Now:

Visit your city planning department or commission. Investigate what building rehabilitation programs are going on in your community. Go to a building-trades union to ask about solar-oriented construction, training, and apprenticeships. In school take sheet-metal and welding courses; drafting, carpentry, woodworking and wood-finishing classes.

### Job Opportunities:

City planner, boiler repairman, painter, rehabilitation-builder, structure retrofitter, cabinet worker, sheet metal worker, plasterer, carpenter: AT philosophy can be followed by any of these skilled workers.

# CHAPTER 5

## AT IN THE REFUSE DUMP



AFTER WORLD War II America became a "throwaway" society. Use it; throw it out; make another; wrap it up; throw it away; throw the wrapping away; buy more; use it; throw it away. . . . Then thinking people became aware of an indisputable fact: There was no more "away" to throw it to!

Household garbage (including cans, paper product packaging, bottles, foils, TV-dinner trays) makes a continuous mountain of waste. Other discards such as old bedsprings, near-empty paint buckets, children's highchairs, and seam-ruptured mattresses add to a growing pile that numbers millions of tons in miscellaneous refuse tossed out daily by American homemakers. Figures compiled in 1970 show Americans junk seven million cars a year, 100 million tires, 20 million tons of paper, and hundreds of millions of cans and bottles. What does one do with it all?

In the decade of the '80s, the massive pile of junk and garbage keeps increasing. Just to collect the garbage cost $2.8 billion ten years ago. "The current figure is four and a half billion dollars a year for municipalities to pay for collecting and disposing of garbage," Dr. Neil Seldman, a Washington, D. C., recycling expert declares. "That estimate is expected to double by 1985. Now we're looking for approximately ten billion dollars to come out of local budgets by 1985."

Dr. Seldman is co-director of the Institute for Local Self-Reliance, based in the nation's capital. According to Seldman, it was the packaging explosion following the Second World War that triggered the refuse problem. Other factors that have created the inordinate municipal mess that causes fiscal headaches for city and county officials may include the demise of the junk man who formerly made curbside purchases of cast-off materials such as iron scrap, newspapers, and rags; the built-in obsolescence in household items; and the throwaway mentality fostered in an affluent society.

Garbage-crammed barges have long been a familiar sight as they head out to sea past the Statue of Liberty in the New York harbor, on their way to the horizon where, out of sight of land, they dump their loads. But the garbage has slowly been coming back on the tides to New England shores.

San Francisco contracted with the peninsula town of Mountain View, paying it two dollars per ton to accept 2,000 tons of solid waste a day. When Mountain View's lowlands were filled, the contract was closed. San Francisco is seeking other dumping grounds. Landfills coast to coast are crammed with refuse to overflowing.

As ridiculous as it may seem, millions of dollars can be realized by recycling this waste that is being covered over in landfills. A veritable treasure for our small world, and a sizable daily deposit for the First Natural Bank of Spaceship Earth is truly going to waste.

With no more "away" available, some AT activists are working hard to turn the waste into a resource. Among them are Dr. Seldman and his colleague Dr. Daniel Knapp. Both are recycling purists. They would like to be called "resource recovery people," but they feel that other so-called recyclers who are actually disposal technicians have co-opted the term.

According to Drs. Seldman and Knapp, when garbage and other assorted refuse is picked up in your neighborhood, it is usually compacted by a specially designed truck to take up less space in transit. The garbage truck may take its load directly to the dump or landfill. More often, it will take it to a transfer station where it is further compacted, reloaded, and taken to a site perhaps as far away as 40 or 50 miles.

Everything is crushed together: vegetable cans, glass wine bottles, aluminum and steel, brass and iron, paint and solvents, flammables and toxics, poisons and plastics. If the dump site is a landfill, when filled it will probably be used for some kind of development, most often homes. When it rains, water leaches through the mass, collecting poisons and toxics on its way toward a riverbed or the sea.

Dan Knapp, author of a small publication titled, "Gone Today, Here Tomorrow," is emphatic about the fallacy of trying to get rid of a problem by barging it or trucking it to some far-off place. "It is a myth," he says, "that you are going to be able to deal with this stuff by taking it out of town. It will eventually get back."

Both Seldman and Knapp also take a dim view of certain methods other than landfill. They cite the huge $73 million plant at Hempstead, New York. This facility burns 4,000 tons of garbage per week and generates 2 million kilowatts of electricity, enough power to run 14,300 homes for a week.

To a casual observer, this would seem outstanding. But not to Knapp and Seldman. "It is a mass-disposal burn plan, a mixed-waste resource energy recovery system through which solid waste is fed directly into a form of combustion system to recover energy," says Seldman. Everything is dumped into a fire pit, burned at high heat, and the heat is used to produce steam to turn electric turbines.

The history of these large plant systems is rather mediocre, according to Seldman. "Federal and state governments have spent about half a billion dollars of public money to develop this technology over the past decade. Currently there are two successful plants." These plants, called waterwall incinerators, are located in Nashville, Tennessee and Saugus, Massachusetts. The Nashville plant disposes of 560 tons per day, and the Saugus incinerator burns 1,200 tons per day.

They are no more than big boilers with water pipes surrounding the fire pit. The garbage and other materials are burned with a fossil-fuel supplement at extremely high heat. Steam is created in the pipes around the fire pit, hence the name "waterwall." The resultant residue ash is processed to remove ferrous materials and is finally deposited elsewhere—usually in a landfill.

This is a costly technology, according to the purists. Despite the governmental investments, only 1 percent of the 150 million tons per year in solid waste generated by America's consumers is handled by the big plants. On the other hand, 7.7 percent is handled by recyclers. There is an inequity in this. "The capital invested in the recycling system over the past decade has been two million dollars," states Neil Seldman. "Five hundred million has been invested in the big plants, and fifty-five percent of that is subsidized by one federal program or other."

Both Seldman and Knapp can document that by recycling materials, more energy is conserved than that created through burning waste, at roughly one one-hundredth of the capital cost. They feel that the 7.7 percent payback in the solid waste stream for the $2 million invested far outshadows the 1 percent payback from the $500 million investment.

"The recycling industry is now rather sophisticated," Seldman states. "Two hundred and fifty municipalities have separate programs. Ten years ago there were one or two."

But none of these advances are without a certain amount of frustration, Seldman is quick to point out. "Recycling is ineligible for government funds. In other words, if you want to buy garbage, you can get a commercialization grant, price support, a whole array of programs—but none of these will allow recycling to take place. If you recycle, you save energy. But you can get no energy entitlement credit. You can only get it if you burn garbage."

Despite these problems, a network of recyclers is being formed across the country. "Five states have recycling associations," Seldman recounts. "Nebraska formed their first in 1980. Michigan is forming up, so is New Jersey. New York State, while it does not have a recycling association, has its county environmental managers who are in effect serving that purpose. New York City has its association, and California has its solid waste management board."

Both Seldman and Knapp are eager to speak out about their technology. "We now know how to collect recyclable materials from your households. We have the trucks. We have processing and training programs. We have intermediary yards. And we have the market. We know how to handle materials, how to crush glass. We know how to get householders to participate. We know how to get kids in school into recycling."

Dan Knapp thinks 70 percent of the materials in garbage dumps is recyclable. Dr. Knapp has worked in big-plant burn operations. He has also worked as a scavenger in a local landfill operation. It is in the latter role that he formed very positive opinions about each.

While working at the Eugene, Oregon, burn facility, where a huge Allis-Chalmers plant has been operating on a spasmodic off-and-on schedule, Knapp realized that this very complicated technology was headed for disaster. The system used is known as "dry shredding." Aluminum, ferrous materials, and other supposedly nonflammable materials are removed in a front-end recovery process. "In the separation, the light materials go up through the top, the heavier drop below. It separates the ferrous, which is the lowest grade material and the least valuable in the solid-waste recovery system. But the aluminum and much of the high-value material goes to the landfill after being shredded, which makes it more difficult to recover if you did want it."

In the process materials must be screened, but the chicken-wire and screen-door-type screening does not remove radioactive materials, and toxic materials go through undetected, according to Knapp. And there is the ever-present danger of explosion because of the dust accumulation and spontaneous combustion. "We told them about this," Knapp said. "However, because of pressures to get the plant into operation, they didn't listen to us. Three months later, it blew up, as we had predicted."

A widely read story in the print medium says, ". . . 250 garbage-and-energy plants are operating outside the United

States, most of them in Europe, many of them problem free for 20 years." Knapp and Seldman refute this. Each can document cases in Europe and Canada where plants have blown up exactly as the one did in Eugene, Oregon.

Dan Knapp's scavenging experience in Berkeley, California, at the Resource and Recovery Depot showed him the benefits of that recycling system. In Berkeley, dumping fees bring in from two to three thousand dollars per day. "But none of the money is being used to support recycling, unfortunately," he admits.

Recyclers are allowed unofficially on the Berkeley dump site despite Environmental Protection Agency (EPA) rulings. "Landfill scavenging is very controversial in landfill circles," laughs Knapp. "It's not practiced very much. But if you're not going to allow scavenging, you're not going to have recycling at a landfill."

He describes how metals are separated by hand, detaching brass from iron, aluminum from steel. Welding torches, big loppers for slicing through bolts, sledges, and pry bars are all part of the scavengers' equipment as they go from truckload to truckload of garbage. Practiced eyes quickly sort out and segregate worthwhile materials that are headed for oblivion. Quickly they are snatched by the scavengers and set aside for recycling.

Recyclers working with the Berkeley Resource and Recovery Depot are quite successful in undertaking a job that could easily be neglected. Five workers, two of them women, recycle about 130 tons of garbage per month. "Total cash flow from the operation, including selling secondhand things as well as scrap, comes to about fifty-five hundred dollars per month for five workers," Knapp told us. "A lot of things can be salvaged if you have the people to do it."

So here is a career opportunity: to start your own business as a recovery technologist.

An area of salvage neglected by most automobile owners is "re-refining" used crankcase oil. Re-refined oil performs as well as virgin oil, experts agree; used oil need not be thrown away. According to DOE officials, if all of our approximately 1.4 billion gallons of used oil could be collected and re-refined every year, 250 million gallons of imported crude could be saved. This is enough to change the oil in 1.5 million cars every day.

The demise of the full-service gas station has put the responsibility of oil changing on the individual. The used oil ends up in the garbage collection, or in many cases is flushed down the storm drain. Often it is spread to kill weeds and succeeds in poisoning the soil.

Some communities and industries pour their used oil on dirt and gravel roads as a dust suppressive. Rains wash the oil into roadside ditches; groundwater action pollutes surrounding land. The lead, additives, heavy metals, and other toxic materials found in used oil create health hazards when dumped into landfills. When used automotive oil is burned as a cheap heating oil, the contaminants are released into the air and add their share to the growing air-pollution problem.

Federal agencies and a few states are passing laws to keep oil out of the dumps. Maryland, Utah, Oregon, Wisconsin, New York, and Minnesota have enacted strict measures. In California, where over 2,000 gas stations, auto stores, repair shops and recycling centers serve as collection sites, an oil recycling plan saved over 3 million gallons in 1980.

An educational effort is taking place slowly throughout

the country to awaken people to the mess that has been created in the American sector of the spaceship, and to cure the citizen/passengers of the "throw-it-away" habit. AT activists are working hard in that direction.

For You to Do Now:

Visit your local solid-waste landfill or refuse dump; inquire about their recycling program. If there is none, you may wish to start one with your friends. Collect aluminum cans, newspapers, and bottles for recycling and extra cash.

Job Opportunities:

Garbage collector, solid waste technician, junk sorter, recycler: men and women work in these areas.

# CHAPTER 6
# AT
# IN
# THE
# SEWER



THERE IS a fortune in silver and gold to be salvaged from the nation's sewers. A U. S. Geological Survey taken in 1976 showed sludge contained 500 parts per million of silver and 30 ppm of gold. Sludge is the solid material remaining after waste water has been extracted. With monetary values in both precious metals skyrocketing, city officials as well as industrialists who use gold and silver are becoming interested in recovery.

In little more than one year the city of Palo Alto, California, where Kodak and Hewlett-Packard have installations that use large quantities of the glittering ore, has earned more than $250,000 in "sifting muck" from municipal sewers.

This is just a drop in the vast waste-water bucket that is filled by the nation's sewer lines. Untold riches in recyclable water and resources flow through underground pipes on their way to the sea or some inland body of water. On its way, this wasted wealth may poison freshwater supplies, or kill irreplaceable species of aquatic life. Hidden in the waste water that wends its poisonous way toward some outlet are nutrients as well as precious metals. When recycled, these nutrients can become the start of another valuable resource instead of depleting an already fragile aquatic food chain.

Two young men solved the problem of reconstituting waste water, and the rewards are available to anyone—individual or government—with the vision to follow their method:

On a cold, rainy November Saturday morning in San Jose, California, in 1969 the laundromat was almost deserted. The only warmth in the starkly white room came from the machines, and only a few were in operation. Graduate students Dominick Mendola and Steven Serfling, both in their mid-twenties, perched on the tops of adjoining clothes driers. "It was the most comfortable place in the building," Mendola recalls. "And it only proves the seat of knowledge functions best when well warmed."

Mendola had obtained his B. S. degree in zoology in 1967; Serfling the same, one year later. Both were interested in aquatic ecology. On this particularly dreary morning the conversation between wash-and-dry cycles turned to the detergent-laden waste water each was sending into the Santa Clara County sewers.

Toxic effluent and its effect on undersea life in south San Francisco Bay had long been the subject of numerous college seminars they had attended as undergraduates. They knew of the poisons discharged over nature's aquatic fish and bivalve nurseries. Together, while their own washing detergents made soiled campus clothes whiter than white, Mendola and Serfling traced an imagined trail from wash cycle to bay outflow. They visualized a small crab or shrimp struggling for a final gasp of oxygen before it succumbed, the last of its hatch. "There has to be a better way," Dominick Mendola declared.

Today Mr. Mendola is vice president and director of operations of Solar AquaSystems, Inc.; Dr. Steve Serfling is SAS president. Together they founded the company. Solar AquaSystems, virtually conceived in the heat of a laundromat drier, is perhaps the world's foremost method for transforming the lowest aftereffects of human civilization into products that are energy and food producing, cost effective, job and career generating, and ecologically sound. Through a patented process Mendola and Serfling are able to change domestic and industrial sewage into pure, potable (drinkable without chlorine additives) water.

The by-products of the system include methane gas, which can be used for space heating; can be containerized for sale; can be used to run turbines for electric power generation; and can be made into methanol. Fertilizer, sterilized and bagged for sale or used on-site, is another by-product. Others include several species of edible fish, prawns, lobsters, and escargot (edible snails). Vegetation biomass is used for composting, methanol production, and fodder for livestock. Finally, a purified water return for irrigation, recreation, industrial, and domestic uses is realized. Employment potential ranges from unskilled labor to the highest technological professional level.

SAS did not spring full grown from the minds of its founders. Years of research and practical experience were tallied before the project was ready for evaluation. Steven Serfling received his master's degree in aquatic ecology from San Diego State University in 1972 and his doctorate from the University of California, Davis.

Dominick Mendola followed his master's with several years of diversified work in the field: oceanographic engineer at Scripps Institute in La Jolla, California; aquatic pollution chemist at the Naval Undersea Research Center and in the sea grant lobster project at San Diego State; Aquaculture Systems Design Specialist for the Syntex Corporation, Palo Alto, California. At this last post Mendola designed a 20-acre **freshwater shrimp farm**, as well as intensive, controlled environmental aquatic systems. He has been a part-time director of the New Alchemy Institute's western aquacultural research projects and the Aquatic Resources Institute.

It was this accumulated expertise Mendola and Serfling brought together when in 1973 they formed Solar Aquafarms, Inc., an agricultural firm specializing in the biological recycling of aquatic waste nutrients in controlled environment systems for the production of freshwater shrimp, fish, and high-protein aquatic plants.

Later, in July, 1976, Serfling directed the formation of Solar AquaSystems, Inc., to concentrate solely on the research, design, and engineering of low technology systems of waste-water reclamation, using the same ecological techniques as Aquafarms. As noted, Dominick Mendola came aboard as vice president.

Conventional sewage treatment processes produce a "secondary effluent"; this method has been adequate with no major changes for over fifty years. Now, however, old-fashioned methods are unable to meet present Federal Water Pollution Control Act criteria without extensive modification, additions, and high construction expense.

Mendola calls conventional sewage treatment systems—the kind you may have in your city—"costly to operate, with high electrical demands; they consume precious natural resources, including fossil fuels, chemicals, and water." Secondary treatment processes, furthermore, are incapable of removing or detoxifying the majority of the most harmful components in modern day waste water: pesticides, herbicides, phenols, heavy metals, and a host of complex domestic and industrial chemicals now recognized as potentially carcinogenic.

"In contrast," Mendola states, "biological lagoon systems containing plant components have proven capable of doing this." The biological lagoon system, with variations, is the key factor in Solar AquaSystems. SAS converts raw sewage into 99 percent pure tertiary effluent through several additional steps. The secret is found in solar heat and covered, insulated greenhouses. Tropical water plants, with artificial habitats for shrimp, fish, lobsters, and other invertebrates, complete the natural process.

When Mendola first spoke with civic groups about harvesting edible seafood from sewage he was met with looks of distaste, audible groans, and considerable negative audience reaction. He soon learned to play down the "influent" phase and stress the "effluent"; but the term still received squeamish disapproval. So the words "waste water" have been universally accepted as a suitable euphemism to placate a sensitive public. Factually, materials discarded through a sewage system, whether starting at kitchen drain, flush toilet, bathtub and shower, industrial fluid waste, or public rest rooms in towering office buildings, all go to the same place: the inflowing pipe at the municipal or regional treatment plant.

Despite the general public's wish to "flush and forget," raw sewage is a precious commodity—but not in its secondary effluent stage. The conventional method takes influent materials through only two processes before they are discharged into some convenient outflow: a river that passes through town, an inland lake, or an oceanic bay.

If the passing river's flow is swift enough it will distribute the toxic elements downstream, perhaps to a neighboring town or city. If it is a slowly moving stream, toxic materials and heavy metals will build up at the outflow pipe. Local fish and wildlife will die, and the stream will become polluted.

Secondary effluent is full of nutrients as well as toxics. Should the treatment plant's outflow pipe, or canal, terminate in an inland lake, algae will grow rapidly, fed by the nutrients, taking all the available oxygen from the water. With the help of toxic poisons, the algae will kill off all wildlife within its shores. A case in point is Lake Erie, a comparatively large freshwater body, which has been slowly struggling back to life after having been "killed" by pollution.

San Francisco's huge oceanic bay, teeming with bottom-dwelling crabs, tiny bay shrimp, oysters, and other succulent seafoods only 40 years ago, now lies moribund. Only the steady freshwater stream from the San Joaquin-Sacramento delta keeps a wide fish highway open for the spawning salmon, steelhead, and striped bass that annually head for foothill nests.

However, the exploding communities of the vast central valley of California are pouring billions of gallons of secondary effluent daily through the delta into the bay. Fish counts have been noticeably lower in recent years along the valley's main rivers. Therefore the necessity for designs such as Solar AquaSystems is evident wherever communities strive for ecological balance in coming years.

Once developed, the process seems relatively simple.

Raw sewage is received through standard underground pipes and is allowed to settle in covered lagoons for several days, as in a conventional treatment plant. Sludge is digested biologically. This is called primary treatment. Pure water is introduced through the self-contained source, sludge is separated for further treatment, and primary waste water continues on into the first of a series of "solar Aquacells," where secondary treatment takes place.

In a conventional process, biochemical oxydizing agents are added, the waste water is agitated and aerated, often trickled through filters, more sludge is removed, the water is chemically treated and discharged as secondary effluent. Nutrients that could cause algae growth, heavy metals, toxic materials such as herbicides and pesticides, and industrial chemicals all wash out into the world food chain.

The Solar AquaSystem begins where conventional means cease. After passing the secondary effluent through a SAS ozone chamber for purification, two more tertiary steps follow, during which the dissolved nutrients feed the plant life and varieties of underwater animal life in the AquaCells. It is through these tertiary treatments that SAS excites enthusiasm in civic futurists.

The physical structure of SAS installations differs from other treatment systems as well. The usual municipal sewage plants cover many acres—they consist of an array of round, open-air lagoons, complicated mazes of steel and concrete pipes, aeration ponds where water is sprayed, covered concrete tanks. Often the conventional system is hidden behind high walls. Several times a month putrid odors are emitted. Sometimes set in green parklike surroundings, the grounds are seldom open to the public.

In contrast, a planned SAS installation includes a verdant park with picnic tables. Small lakes are dotted with sailboats and canoes. There are running streams with pure, clear water meandering between the lakes, and several windmills generate more electrical power. A pumping station helps distribute the water. Bike trails, nature walks, and jogging tracks wind throughout the area. A housing development might border some of the small lakes. A golf course, soccer field, or playground may be included. The air would be fresh and smell of greenery and flowers.

In a central site a group of white-covered greenhouse AquaCells are placed with orderly precision. Inside the greenhouses technicians monitor water temperatures, constantly check for impurities, and supervise the seafood tanks. These technicians inspect the underwater environment in the huge 8-feet-deep tanks used in the tertiary treatment. They remove weak or undersize fish, sort out crustaceans according to length and weight. The air and water temperatures are constant, winter and summer. It is a pleasant place for anyone to work. The air is perfumed by water hyacinth blossoms, which spread a carpet of color over the tank tops.

A light-industry section has been set aside for trucks to on-load sludge materials for fertilizer manufacturing; these processes are performed at the solid-waste facility not far away. There is no odor from sewage or sludge, for the anaerobic digestive system has removed all odor-producing bacteria under cover of the solar-heated, air-insulated Aqua-Cell greenhouses.

Aquatic plant materials, harvested daily, are ground up for hog and cattle feed, after first having been treated along with the sludge for heavy-metal recovery. Some of the organic materials are retained for sale as garden mulch and composting. The remainder are converted into methane gas and methanol fuel (alcohol) for on-site uses or sold and shipped into the market. At another section, fish and shellfish are harvested, iced down, packaged for on-site sale, or shipped to wholesale distributors. All electrical energy is generated on-site with windmills, solar photovoltaic collectors, and methane gas supplying the source.

In short, not one ounce of the raw sewage discharge (influent) is wasted. More important: a sizable daily deposit is recorded at the First Natural Bank. The self-sustaining wastewater treatment, exactly counter to the conventional method, uses no fossil fuel, no outside electricity, no natural gas, no fresh water, and a comparatively small amount of steel, concrete, and other building materials in its design.

Truck drivers, gardeners, boat handlers, custodians, greenskeepers, clerks, security, chemists, technicians: all are employed by the solar sewage treatment plant. Their wages are derived from marketing by-products, from recreational fees; of course, existing sewer bond indebtedness and future lines and hookups would follow usual procedures. The system itself is tax free and self-sustaining once in operation.

SAS productivity potential is outstanding. On a year-round basis at the ratio of 2 acres of AquaCells per 1 MGD (10,000) waste-water depositors, when temperatures are held between 20 degrees C and 30 degrees C (68–88° F) through solar and site-generated heat sources, up to 50,000 tons of underwater creatures—daphnia, detritivores, amphipods, macrophytes, snails, etc.—are harvested to add to organic fertilizers and animal chows.

Tons of vegetable matter from fast-growing aquatic plants are harvested daily. The water hyacinth doubles its growth every twenty-four hours, thus making it a prime product under controlled conditions. The value of this by-product has yet to be totally realized, because its uses are so varied. However, if consumed entirely as a source of methanol automotive fuel, the value per acre ascends many times over comparative grain crops. Absence of growing, fertilizing, and harvesting costs alone bears out this theory, still to be tested in this fast-changing energy era.

Edible food production is even more important. Over 10,000 pounds of fish and 5,000 pounds of shrimp can be grown each year on each acre of AquaCells. Add to this the millions of fish that can be raised in nearby hatcheries for sport and food in SAS-fed lakes and streams. Where ocean-run streams and rivers are nearby, new hatches of salmon, striped bass, and steelhead can be introduced. In bass and catfish country, new small lakes can be designed to accept fingerlings; old, tired lakes can be brought back to life.

Is this some hazy, futurist dream? Not at all. The SAS method is in production, as are other scientific waste-water reclamation systems. Is this conservationist method being accepted? Unfortunately, not readily. Sanitary engineers in many cases do not wish to investigate or research any other than conventional methods. Health department people are often unresponsive. County, state, and municipal elected officials steer clear. Ordinary citizens are not aware.

Nevertheless, this new way of recycling water formerly lost, and getting positive rewards in return, is slowly catching on. For example, there's Hercules City, California, which lies on the south shore of San Pablo Bay, a part of San Francisco's North Bay, 30 miles from the city. A small but fast-growing, planned community, Hercules City is flanked by oil refineries storage tanks, and mushrooming home development. The city of Hercules' waste water had been treated by the neighboring community of Pinole, but this plant capacity was exceeded in 1980.

As part of its overall long-term plans for developing an environmentally sound, model community in an area of water shortages, the city of Hercules opted to construct its own treatment facility which would produce a high-quality effluent for their own reuse, and to market reclaimed water to several local industries. They contracted with SAS to build a series of Solar AquaCells, which were completed in 1979.

A relatively small 10-acre facility, the modular design can be enlarged as the city of Hercules grows. Instead of using the harvested water hyacinth and duckweed plants that float in the AquaCells for methane gas, Hercules preferred to reuse them in the form of compost, needed in large quantities for landscaping purposes during development of their community over the next twenty years.

Two local industries requiring water quality "close to the quality of the original tap water" will buy all they can get from the treatment plant. Also, two creeks winding through the community, often dry most of the year, are being "enhanced" and incorporated into a marsh-wildfowl sanctuary.

Instead of hauling sludge to out-of-town dump sites, as is done by most neighboring conventional treatment plants, 100 percent of all solids are recycled directly within the community. Assuming sale of only 50 percent of the reclaimed water at 50 percent of the value of tap water, the economic benefit from the sale or use of the reclaimed water to replace imported supplies could, in itself, pay for a major portion of the facility's annual operations and maintenance costs, according to Dominick Mendola.

The cost of conventional, high-technology facilities construction is from two to three times higher than construction of Solar AquaCell process plants. The city of Hercules was recently honored with the state of California Governor's Award for the "most appropriate" technology project of the year. This pleases Mendola and Serfling mightily, but it does not mark an end to their efforts.

"We've recently bid on a one million gallon per day

water hyacinth reclamation system for the city of San Diego," Dominick Mendola told us in the summer of 1980. "We've also installed a small pilot facility for the city of El Paso, Texas. There's a small demonstration for a developer in North County, San Diego, aimed at using the effluent from the treatment system to enhance one of our coastal lagoons." With people like Mendola and Serfling, like Neil Seldman and Dan Knapp, there is a good chance that we will survive our own mess after all. A career in appropriate technology working with refuse and waste water will make a great contribution to this small world.

### For You to Do Now:

Visit your local sewage disposal facility. Determine the degree of purity of the effluent. Find out where the waste water is discharged, and whether or not it is poisoning the environment. Invite your local elected official for a class discussion on waste water.

### Job Opportunities:

Sanitary engineer, chemist, aquatic biologist, sea-food farmer, truck driver: all find their careers in waste-water disposal and reclamation.

# CHAPTER 7
# AT AND CONSERVATION: ENERGY AND ENVIRONMENT



CLAIRE DEDRICK is an active member and former vice president of the Sierra Club. She helped found the Bay Conservation and Development Commission (BCDC) to keep San Francisco Bay alive. "San Francisco Bay was being very poorly treated," she says. "It is a major estuary that has been unprotected for well over one hundred years." She and her husband, Kent, spearheaded a campaign to pass protective legislation.

Claire and Kent Dedrick are friendly, easy-to-know people. He is a mathematical physicist with a doctoral degree;

she has a Ph. D. in microbiology and is a Stanford researcher specializing in immunization. But recently she has become involved with state government. When Gov. Jerry Brown was forming his first administration, he tapped Mrs. Dedrick to head the California Resources Agency. Then, when there was an opening, he named her to the state Public Utilities Commission (PUC). PUC duties include regulation of certain privately owned utilities and transportation companies, and securing for the public service rates that are just and reasonable.

Mrs. Dedrick believes the term "appropriate technology" may become a "buzz word"—a cliché with no meaning. While her entire outlook and experience point to AT thinking, she protests that being lumped in with AT philosophy does not fit. "I am a pragmatist," she told us. "I'm a fixer by nature. I like to make things work. I am not much of a philosopher."

Despite her protests, however, Claire Dedrick made some statements to us that would make any AT activist proud. "As a conservationist, which I have been most of my life, it is screamingly apparent and obvious that this country is in the economic position that it is in, worldwide, because we have thrown away a major resource: we have wasted oil and gas— all petroleum resources. Sold it at prices, frequently government controlled, that were unreasonably low. Promoted waste and reduced that resource to a point where—because we have not changed our way of living—we are dependent on foreign sources for energy."

Energy, Claire Dedrick states, is one of the three fundamental requirements for civilization; the other two are food and water. "And air, of course," she adds quickly, "which no one had argued about before, but sadly, we may run out of that."

Mrs. Dedrick is not a pessimist, however, about the energy situation. She and her colleagues on the PUC are eager to study applications for other modes of energy production, particularly in co-generation, and in small hydro installations. She looks for a vast change in energy production. "In a sense we are lucky," she asserts, "that the high price of oil, this whole business of the international cartel, came at a time when we still have the financial and physical resources to find our own alternatives and to develop our own energy independence. And I don't mean coal."

There is no question that America has thrown away energy. Is still throwing it away. This is evident on every city street where drivers spin rubber and pour the gas into inefficient carburetors, blowing it out the tailpipes in a trail of fumes. It is evident in overheated buildings, or in empty, fully lighted office buildings.

According to research by the Center for Strategic and International Studies, Georgetown University, almost half of the United States energy input goes to waste. The total 1979 energy supply reached 80.8 quads. A quad is a quadrillion (1,000,000,000,000,000) British thermal units (Btu's) of energy. To help place that into perspective, it takes 170 supertankers to haul one quad of oil from the Mideast. There were 16.7 quads from imported oil, and 20.4 quads from domestic oil. Coal contributed 17.8 quads, and 19.8 quads came from natural gas. Only 3.2 quads came from hydroelectric power, and even less, 2.8 quads, came from nuclear power. Geothermal offered a mere .09 quads. Through leakage in the system over 30 quads were wasted. The study showed an avoidable loss of 30 to 40 quads, twice that needed in 1980 to operate all the homes, offices, factories, and vehicles in the United States.

Through more appropriate methods and engineering,

AT activists are zeroing in on the transportation and automotive industries, on agriculture and forestry, to turn those drastic wastes around. A kind of desperation has been registered by many who have been touched personally by another series of events. Two cases stand out: the Three Mile Island near-disaster and the Love Canal tragedy. We will not attempt a postmortem of these two incidents; there has been much written in that regard. However, that these are but two among many less-publicized events underlines the need for dedicated career people trained in technologies that will make these "accidents" impossible.

The whole matter—conservation of the world's energy sources and environment—is stupendous. Health factors, morality aspects, economics—all are involved. It is when economics take precedence over health and morality that troubles most often surface. Scientists disagree about the feasibility of nuclear fission as a nonending energy source. Proponents, led by Dr. Edward Teller, widely referred to as "father of the hydrogen bomb," say the worldwide shortage of energy will increase if the United States ceases to participate in nuclear production. But Teller does not promise complete safety in producing energy from the atom or in disposing of its waste products. "It is nonsense to say anything is completely safe," he says. "Life itself is an incurable disease."

Dr. John W. Gofman, a medical physicist, takes the view opposite to Dr. Teller's. Dr. Gofman fears radiation from nuclear reactors, from physical breakdown as experienced at Three Mile Island, and from radioactive by-products. Such radiation, according to Dr. Gofman, will cause birth defects, kill people with cancer, and deposit radioactive poison in livestock and vegetation that ends up in the food chain.

Dr. Gofman argues from a basis of health and medicine,

as well as economics. "The number of premature deaths caused by the Three Mile Island accident *will be no fewer than six*," Gofman emphasized in his book, *Poisoned Power*. "The number could easily be 60, or 600, for the doses could well be 100 times higher than the government estimates. And all the while, the industry and government officials lie to the American people, saying there was 'no injury to people.'"

Both Gofman and Teller are positive in their respective positions. Both feel their philosophy is correct, that their conclusions are irrefutable. Regardless of the rightness or wrongness of their stands, however, other factors weigh heavily. Proven uranium reserves in the U. S. total only 600,000 tons of yellowcake (uranium 308); to fuel the 700 large American reactors in operation and on the drawing boards would require 7,800,000 tons. Therefore, the so-called "bright hope of mankind" could become swiftly obsolete for lack of fissionable material. Discounting the danger of nuclear war and sabotage of reactors, the unknown as well as the recognized safety problems that surround reactor sites place this technology under the heading "inappropriate."

Potentially as dangerous as radiation is the proliferation of toxic poisons from dump sites. A recent study by the Environmental Protection Agency for the U. S. Senate health subcommittee shows that more than 1.2 million Americans may be exposed to health hazards because they live near toxic waste disposal sites. EPA estimates 30,000 sites may contain a large number and variety of chemicals that could produce cancer, reproductive disorders, and complications of the nervous system, as well as many other illnesses.

There seems to be a question regarding "job" and "career" responsibility for potential environmental danger. Are the electricians who wired Three Mile Island, for instance, responsible for the accident? They were "just doing a job." Are career people like Professor Teller more responsible for the danger? Or the engineers who detailed the work? How about the truck drivers on their way to a landfill with a load of toxic poison? Are they responsible, or their superiors?

Love Canal should never have had its tragedy. But one wonders where the responsibility lies in the area of energy waste. Could we all accept a share? Perhaps nuclear plants will not be necessary if we all become conservationists. After all, the relatively tiny 2.8 quads that nuclear fission has put into the energy grid would hardly be missed if Americans learned to conserve willingly and eagerly.

That, in fact, seems to be happening now. At the time the Georgetown studies were written, a surprising decline in energy consumption was noticed throughout the country. Some specialists have speculated that the United States may now be moving into an extended period of little or no growth in the demand for energy. In 1979 for the first time in more than a quarter century, the demand for energy did not increase.

This decrease in demand can be traced to an unexpected gain in energy efficiency in automobile engine design, the result of technological improvements made in response to higher oil prices. This is not enough, say appropriate technology activists. Improving automobile gasoline mileage is merely the beginning. Their optimum is no gasoline at all! They also see a reduced reliance on conventional fuels for heating homes and businesses. Conservative technology will be practiced on the farm as well as in city homes and work places. Sun power will replace nuclear power; sun power will be used instead of petroenergy: so contend AT people. But they are not completely blinded by the sun.

"Solar does not lead to Nirvana," says Denis Hayes, one of solar power's leading exponents. Hayes is at the same time a realist. Denis Hayes is director of the federally funded Solar Energy Research Institute (SERI). He brought environmental issues into the headlines in 1970 when he organized the first Earth Day. Not the guru type, Hayes is a pleasant, unassuming person who, at thirty-six was perhaps the youngest director of a national research laboratory. His institutional budget for 1980 was $106 million; the laboratory employs 700 researchers.

However, Hayes is frustrated because government is unresponsive to solar. "Right now," he says, "we are spending more money at SERI than will be spent on solar research by all the governments in the world combined. Yet we are having difficulties overcoming the status quo. For instance, we put a lot more into Middle Eastern oil than we do into encouraging use of solar energy."

Pointing out that it is of utmost importance to get the information on solar potential into the hands of the people, not to rely on corporations to promote it, Hayes admits tax incentives may be required to get industry into solar power.

The United States will lead the way toward energy self-reliance in the next century, possibly before. That is the viewpoint of most AT people, including the staff at the Institute for Local Self-Reliance (ILSR). Located in a time-worn brick and stone townhouse in Washington's Adams-Morgan neighborhood, emissaries from this nonprofit corporation reach out into communities nationwide to demonstrate benefits of controlling one's own environment to anyone willing to extend the effort to learn.

The job of teaching self-reliance has not been easy. "There are numerous problems that must be overcome," say ILSR people. "Inadequate information on technical, legal, and organizational alternatives; inadequate hands-on expertise and know-how; a lack of confidence and vision among

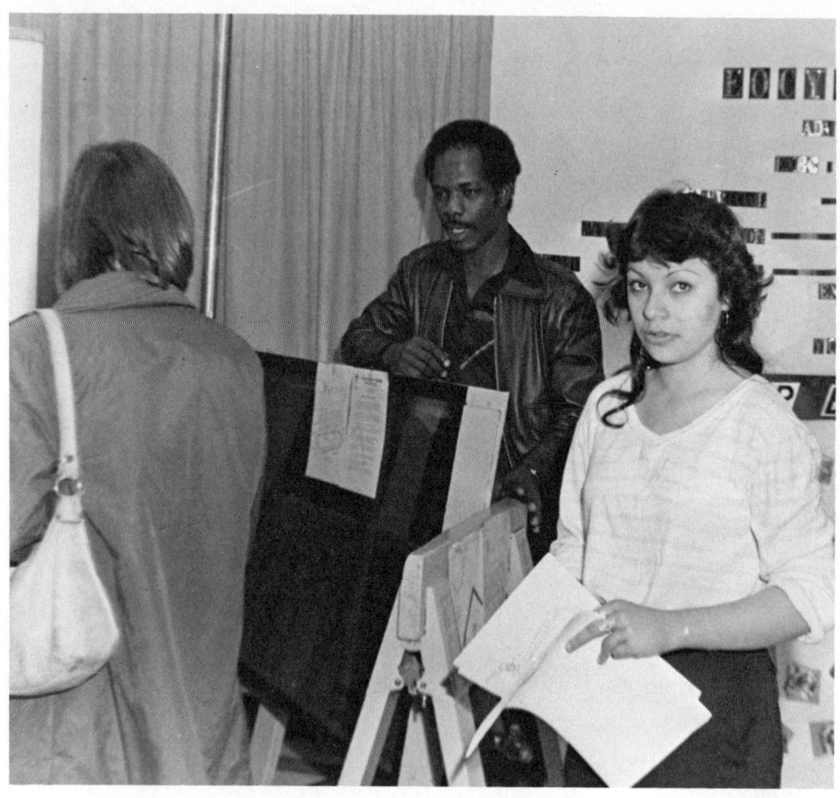

Ronald Mitchell, youth trainee supervisor of the Economic Opportunity Commission, Yolo County, California, explains program to an Energy Show visitor, while Kathy Molyneux, a solar collector trainee, distributes literature. Many employment opportunities are open to young people through various training programs.

both citizens and politicians regarding what could be; public and private sector policies that make local self-reliance impractical or impossible."

A strategy for energy self-reliance addresses all these barriers. Through basic research, neighborhood energy audits, demonstration projects, rooftop greenhouses, solar collector installations, waste-utilization programs, composting sites, and many more activities, these AT teachers show by doing it that their careers are not merely jobs.

The 1980s will be keynoted by many programs to match those of the Institute for Self-Reliance. There will be more aggressive salesmanship by manufacturers of solar equipment. More entrepreneurs will challenge the marketplace with new and more conservative machines and methods. Photovoltaic equipment will be evident on more rooftops. Solar hot-water systems will be added to existing buildings and will be included as a matter of course in new construction.

Retrofitting will become a large industry as homeowners and apartment landlords seek lower heating costs. Code-dictated insulation will be required in all buildings, new and old. Tinkering will be replaced by industrial design in transit and architecture and agriculture.

In each and every facet of conservation, new job and career possibilities will blossom: Every task from sheet-metal work to carpentry to glazing to plumbing will need trained hands and supervisory people—both men and women.

As in any new movement, leaders will spring up along the way. One of these is Chuck Stone, power-alcohol pioneer from tiny Wilton, California. Wilton is a suburban farm community southeast of Sacramento, the state capital. More interesting, Stone's workshop is within sight of Rancho Seco, the Sacramento Municipal Utilities District (SMUD) nuclear reactor. Rancho Seco is a twin of the Three Mile Island plant.

Here among beige-colored oat fields and dairy farms Chuck Stone converts anything cellulose—wood chips, urban waste, agricultural residues—into alcohol to replace gasoline. Such is Stone's success that his company, Future Fuels of

America, Inc., has contracted with the Bank of America, the world's largest banking institution, to prepare a fleet of cars (1980 Ford Granadas, Couriers, and Liberators) to run on what Chuck Stone calls "methanol-X" a 100 percent alcohol fuel.

Alcohol for automobile combustion is not new. Early cars, such as Henry Ford's Model-T, were designed to use alcohol as fuel. But the low cost of gasoline in comparison with alcohol soon made it the drivers' favorite. Other countries, notably Brazil, are far ahead of the United States in power-alcohol usage. Brazil, a nation of 123 million people and 8 million autos, plans to have 2 million alcohol-powered cars on the road by 1985, including older models with converted engines.

Gasohol—10 percent alcohol, 90 percent gasoline—is widely sold in the midwestern Corn Belt states. AT purists, however, scoff at using any gasoline at all. Simple conversions costing less than $100 will allow any internal combustion engine to run more cleanly and efficiently on pure alcohol than on gasoline mixtures.

Power alcohol comes under two separate chemical headings: ethanol (ethyl alcohol) and methanol (methyl alcohol). Ethanol is produced by "brewing" or distilling grains and other sugar or starch-containing produce. One ton of wheat grain yields about 85 gallons of alcohol under normal conditions. Methanol is made from gas, which emanates from decaying biomass (vegetable fibers). Natural gas from petroleum fields and from coal can also be made into methanol. Wood chips, when pyrolized—superheated to combustion—give off natural gases that can be converted to methanol. Tapioca, the same source for pudding desserts, is an excellent source for ethanol, as are sugarcane waste, molasses, sugar beets, maize, rice, and a few dozen other food stocks.

AT people frown on using farm-grown food produce for power-alcohol production. The energy used in planting, growing, and harvesting these crops is a poor trade-off for the good that may come from its value as a replacement fuel. The use of food products for power energy, although the mash residue can be used as an animal feed supplement, seems a waste while millions of the passengers on Spaceship Earth face starvation. Conservationists would use the waste engendered within cities, the trash and garbage that choke America's alleys and landfills, as a source for alcohol.

Alcohols are the answer to keeping U. S. wheels turning, according to Professor Richard K. Pefley, head of the University of Santa Clara Department of Mechanical Engineering. Dr. Pefley is another who observes the world as a spacecraft; he sees liquid fuels derived from the sun. His work with alcohol fuel, which has been going on for twelve years, concludes that "methyl alcohol from coal offers a liquid energy alternative to gasoline for automotive and possible diesel use, and shows considerable promise for supplanting petroleum in the latter part of this century."

AT activists look with foreboding on such statements. They take a longer view, one that does not include coal. As environmentalists, they fear giving high priority to coal mining without first laying out guidelines about how mining sites should be preserved, the safety conditions under which coal is mined, and finally the method used in extracting alcohol fuel from coal.

The federal government, after long delays, began a massive synthetic fuel program with the signing of the Energy Security Act of 1980 by President Jimmy Carter on July 4 of that year. Billions of dollars in public money will have been put on the line in an effort to turn the nation's abundant coal deposits into gas and liquid fuels.

However, major environmental and economic questions will arise from that effort, as large numbers of workers and their families will be moved into the western regions where most of the coal and oil-shale deposits are located. State and local governments will have difficult decisions to make. Roads, fire protection, water, security, and other services will be required by the companies and their miners. While much of the cost will be paid by private enterprise, taxpayers and consumers will pay the greatest amount.

Avowed conservationists feel that if the land were managed properly, enough vegetation could be produced to furnish biomass for the world's energy needs. However, agricultural engineers such as Vashek Cervinka, a long-range planner for the California Food and Agricultural Department, see the farmer as an integral part in future power-alcohol production. Farmers would contract with large companies producing alcohol just as they contract with canneries for tomatoes and beans.

Literally hundreds of private citizens are setting up small backyard stills, cooking up gallons of vegetable wastes and brewing their own alcohol. The purists, in these cases, use only solar heat to ferment their mash. A good description of this process is found in *Methanol and Other Ways Around the Gas Pump*, by John Lincoln. *Mother Earth News* and several other publications have similar plans for solar fermentation.

Vashek Cervinka is bemused by these backyard distillers. "The question is economics," he will tell you. "For how much can you produce it? And how much time can you spend on it?" Cervinka puts home solar stills in the hobby category.

David Owens, of Oxnard, California, does not agree. Owens, an engineer, has perfected a solar method of home distilling that he says will furnish 350 gallons of ethanol alcohol per month at a cost of 20 cents per gallon. Owens powers his car, heats his house, and runs an electric generator on ethanol. He has published a work manual that gives all the details of producing ethanol from vegetable wastes, cornstalks, and garbage throwaways from your neighborhood vegetable market.

Owens is particularly strong on community participation in ethanol production. His stills, made easily by the average unskilled person, can be shared in a neighborhood with one backyard, a vacant section of a lot, or an empty service station. His method, which can be run completely by solar power during daylight hours, or on a twenty-four-hour basis with a simple heater setup, needs no technical supervision.

Ethanol, according to Owens, runs cooler than gasoline, is cleaner on internal engine parts, and gives off pure carbon dioxide when exploded in an engine. No catalytic converter is required, and for a few cents two carburetor jets can be obtained to interchange with factory originals; the system is then reversible should the car operator wish to shift back and forth between gasoline and ethanol.

If it is that simple, why hasn't it been done before? "That's the question I asked myself when I started working on this," Owens answers. "But it works, and that's the most important thing about it." And so the fluid-energy debate goes on.

Meanwhile, other hobbyists create perpetual motion machines. One of these is Bill Lucas, a Texas inventor, who claims his "gravity machine" is ready for mass production. A clanking mixture of wheels, bicycle chains, concrete weights, and an old Toyota gearbox produces enough power to activate a 400-watt electric generator, according to Lucas. His weird machine cost him $4,000 in spare parts, and once started will run to eternity, or as long as the parts hold up.

While Bill Lucas's perpetual motion machine might take a waiting world by surprise, a more current source for power is found in photovoltaic cells. A photovoltaic (PV) material, usually silicon, is something that generates electricity when placed in sunlight. Direct sunlight on treated silicon produces enough electricity to run, by direct current, such equipment as motors, appliances, cameras, computers, lights, and radios; it can charge storage batteries.

The familiar giant, flat arms extending from earth satellites hold panels of solar PV cells; energy is collected to power equipment on board. Until recently, PV cells were very expensive, and so was the elctricity produced: five dollars to fifteen dollars per cell/watt. However, mass production and improved technology have brought the cost down; soon PV power will be competitive with other forms, approximately thirty cents per watt.

The world's biggest PV system was dedicated in June, 1980, at Natural Bridges National Monument, Utah. It replaces diesel generators that required 15,000 gallons of oil per year to provide electricity for six residences, maintenance facilities, the visitors' center, and a water sanitation system. The 7,600-acre park is the site of three of the world's largest sandstone bridges.

The PV array collects enough solar electricity to charge a huge 112-cell lead-acid battery from which the installation draws its nighttime power. The PV system has a top output of 100 kilowatts at noon on clear days. However, even under cloudy conditions it generates some power, according to Pete Parry, park superintendent. Total cost of the system, which includes 266,029 solar cells, was $3 million. It was not intended to be a cost saver, but was designed to further technological advances of alternate energy systems. Future installations in national parks will be less expensive.

The Lawrence Livermore Laboratory (LLL) in the San Francisco South Bay area has been working to perfect PV solar cells made of a sandwich of thin films containing cadmium sulfide and copper sulfide. These cells can be mass produced at a lower cost than silicon cells. However, the thinner materials are not as durable as needed for general use. And the cell is not as efficient as theory predicted, according to LLL scientists. In striving to overcome these problems, they are testing a "sputtering" method of making the thin films that may improve the stability and efficiency of the cells. The addition of a little zinc may also increase efficiency, if all goes as planned at LLL.

To demonstrate the performance and reliability of PV solar cells, LLL has designed what they call their Solar Surrey. This small battery-driven three-wheeler, designed in the mode of a large golf cart, has for its roof an array of PV cells. These keep its battery pack recharged as long as the sun shines.

While it is easy to dismiss the Solar Surrey as a plaything, its importance to the automotive industry has not gone unnoticed. Designers are working on prototypes using PV electric power as a backup to conventional battery-electric and alcohol-powered internal combustion (IC) engine hybrids. These systems are both IC and electric in the same vehicle. Designers think if a sizable array of PV cells could be incorporated, all three systems could work in combination to achieve efficient, inexpensive operation, independent of petroleum.

LLL has two other research projects for which they envision promising results: solar heaters for industrial use.

Solar energy, as we know, can save considerable amounts of energy now used to heat water. Solar collectors on home roof-tops are becoming increasingly common. Dairies, factories, and industrial work places all around the country have made the transition to solar hot-water heating. Now LLL has come up with new designs and methods.

American industry burns the equivalent of 650 million barrels of oil each year to make steam, and another 30 million barrels to heat water. Solar energy could replace most of this fuel if solar collectors and concentrators were less expensive to install. LLL's design for an industrial water heater is a shallow pond that looks like a big waterbed. The plastic bag is 4 meters wide and 60 meters long. It lies between concrete curbs on a pad of insulating glass foam. It is covered with an arched plastic roof.

Shallow ponds are not new as heat collectors. But the LLL idea is the first for contained shallow-pond heating. The plastic-bag enclosure seals the water from evaporation and ground draining. The roof keeps the water from being cooled by wind and reradiation. The glass foam insulates the hot water from the cooling ground surface.

The U. S. Army has proposed that a 6-acre shallow solar pond system be built at Ft. Benning, Georgia. This facility will include over 80 ponds and will supply half a million gallons of hot water per day to the post laundry and two barrack complexes housing 6,500 people. The system will pay for itself within ten to twelve years, according to LLL people, and will be in operation before 1982.

The second LLL project is a solar steam generator. To be successful, solar energy must be concentrated in some way. The problem has been in the extremely high expense of existing concentrating collectors. An inexpensive solar concentrator would save considerable amounts of money and petroenergy.

The LLL system is simple. It is a large inflated cyclinder of thin-film plastic with a clear upper half and an aluminized lower half, which serves as a reflector. This collector, laid flat, surrounds a horizontal pipe that is coated and insulated. Solar energy is concentrated onto the pipe by the reflector. Water passing through the pipe is heated to 170° C (338° F); it can be used as hot water or "flashed" into steam. The steam can be used to turn turbines, generating electricity. Modules 10 meters long are being tested to confirm predictions, and working systems are expected by 1982.

One alternative energy source that takes advantage of conservation at its best is called "co-generation." Co-generation is another technology that is not new; it was widely used in eastern states before 1900, but was phased out with the advent of cheap oil and gas. Co-generation is the process of recovering heat normally lost when electricity is produced and using that heat to help satisfy local energy needs.

"Widespread use of co-generation will result in a productive network of decentralized alternative energy sources," say engineers at Nack and Sunderland, whose comprehensive study of co-generation at the University of California at San Luis Obispo (Cal Poly) has estimated it will save the university a quarter of a million dollars per year. "These sources can generate much needed new energy at one-half to two-thirds the installed cost per kilowatt of new power company generating plants," their study says.

Hot (900° F) gases from turbine exhausts will power a waste-heat boiler to supply the 16,000 pounds per hour of base steam needed for year-round heating and cooling campus buildings. "The co-generator will also produce 72,000 kilowatt hours per day of electricity for sale back to the electric power company," the study continues. "This is more electric power than is typically consumed on campus, thus resulting in a fuel saving to the community and a dollar credit to the university."

Industries nationwide are taking a long hard look at such conservationist practices that could spell energy gains as well as economic gains for their stockholders. Energy- and dollar-conscious citizens are helping to conserve by riding bicycles to work and school. City planners are laying out more and more bike trails terminating at urban centers and designating bike lanes for city streets. But Sol Levine, a Highland Park, Illinois, father has gone one step farther. He has set up a bicycle stand in his living room, hooked the bike up to a generator and a 12-volt automobile battery. His children pump their own power if they wish to watch their favorite television programs. Levine estimates he saves one barrel of crude oil a year through child power.

All the tiny savings—from Sol Levine's bike-tv to backyard solar stills—have had some impact on the total energy picture. According to the Department of Energy, energy consumption in 1979 was slightly less than 1978. By 1990, as some experts see it, oil imports could be cut in half if the decline continues. And that is without a crash program for nuclear power or growth in coal consumption.

This, of course, suits AT activists very well. And the economy need not suffer, they say. Estimates for the number of new jobs attributed to solar installations of all types in the year 1981 is over 500,000. As other technologies in industry and related fields are perfected in the next few years, many more people will get jobs through appropriate technology. And as more jobs come from AT thinking, more lifetime careers will be started.

FOR YOU TO DO NOW:

Take an energy audit of your own home and family automobile. Seek ways to conserve outside-sourced energy; substitute on-site energy: solar, alcohol, wood. Investigate a project in your science class for making power alcohol (methanol, ethanol). Study the concept of photovoltaic solar conversion.

JOB OPPORTUNITIES:

Energy auditor, inventor, agricultural engineer, entrepreneur: careers involving conservation.

# CHAPTER 8
# AT IN INDUSTRY



WE HAVE shown that personal commitment has deep significance in this small world. Recycling, conserving, insulating, gardening, distilling; in home, community, city—individual interest is paramount in AT. Individuality is often submerged under the heavy influence of industrial might. However, we feel that appropriate technology and industry do not constitute a contradiction. What may be needed is some reordering of priorities for industry to fit into the scheme for the '80s and beyond.

Our research in AT has shown us that the giant industrial field that holds the hopes of the American economy is the most unyielding to ecological changes. Unless these changes would show immediately in black ink in the account ledgers, they are best forgotten by what some industrialists call "do-gooder" environmentalists, ecologists, and AT activists.

The building industry is the least willing to change, if our studies are valid. Note the acre upon acre of new housing covering up prime farm land in Pennsylvania, Ohio, Wisconsin, and California, to name a few locations. Venture capital presses for zoning changes in government council chambers nationwide. Developers pay little heed to the hard facts of conservation.

As builders, they face their wide windows northward, making it impossible for the sun naturally and passively to warm interiors. They scrimp on insulation and install inadequate heating and cooling systems. Their interior designs are space wasteful, and their plumbing ignores the progress made in supply and disposal within the last decade.

These houses are not cheap. In the 1981 market they sell for well into the six-figure category. Some less-expensive tract homes go for $70,000 or $80,000. Their builders' thinking is obviously obsolete. John N. Cole, whose informative column appears regularly in Rodale's *New Shelter* magazine, comments on what he refers to as "circular thinking" in shelter design, as well as in everyday living. Cole says that in the past we accepted no limitations. We sought more timberlands when local wood supplies were depleted. We pushed onward in search of minerals, and metals, and croplands. Each was a narrow-scope search. As dwellings became more sophisticated, spaces were designed for only one function: Sleeping, reading, recreation. "A house was a collection of functions,"

Cole writes, "and each was considered in its straight-line, single-purpose dimension."

As we recognize the limits of our resources, we must recalibrate our shelter plans. We must look at every square foot of space, every appliance, every piece of furniture and structural element and ask ourselves how many different and complementary functions every unit can perform. We should no longer accept the notion that any single unit has a single function. Whatever its purpose, it should be extended until it meets itself, until it fulfills a cycle in which next to nothing is wasted and almost everything is utilized.

Shelters for the future must have a circular function. Woodstoves must also heat water and be available for cooking. Fireplaces must circulate air throughout the dwelling and heat water too; they must be designed not to waste heat up drafty chimneys. Greenhouses can add to the larder in winter and also have another function—that of being a warm-air collector for the rest of the house. Landscaping should be designed for shade in summer and allow the sun's rays to penetrate in winter.

The individual making homebuilding a career choice will be well served not to get tied down by obsolete thinking. Other kinds of architecture—office buildings, factories, hospitals—as well as restaurants, dairy farms, and government buildings all need designers with AT background.

A good example of interior-space architecture and design with ecology in mind is found in the rehab of the fifty-year-old Chrysler Building across the street from New York City's Grand Central Station. Here the new headquarters for Dancer Fitzgerald Sample, Inc., a large and successful advertising agency, has drawn its share of attention within its field. The interior design and architectural professions have also taken notice. "What an office for the '80s should be is open to debate," says *Interiors* magazine in its December, 1979, issue, "but one thing is sure: it should be energy efficient."

Within 21,000 square feet the firm of Prentice & Chan, Ohlhausen fashioned work room for nearly 900 DFS employees who must function in a creative, businesslike manner without crowding or being inhibited by the closed-in feeling typical of many offices. Within the H-shaped building private offices were placed around the windowed perimeter; the natural daylight helps conserve electricity; all windows open for ventilation. Portable lamps take the place of ceiling fixtures, and Owens-Corning Solar-screen is tracked across all windows in public spaces and in some private offices too. The power wattage is relatively low: 4½ watts per square foot.

This kind of building "recycling" is going on all over the country. Architecture and interior design students are learning quickly that the better way includes AT.

Another advanced design—a showcase in Sacramento, California—shows new ideas in the works for professional office buildings. A huge state building designed by Sim Van der Ryn and his staff when he was state architect will be finished by 1981 on a block-square site two blocks from the State Capitol. It is the world's first and largest solar office building, according to Van der Ryn. If it succeeds, as its designers say it will, it could revolutionize the industry.

From the street it looks like any other structure. As you withdraw a short distance into a park across the street, the perspective changes and through the trees you see inset windows and overhangs not visible from sidewalk level. A vast atrium in the middle of the building is covered by a series of louvered skylights that can be used for nighttime cooling or daytime heat collection. A large bed of rocks in the atrium absorbs or gives off heat, depending on the season. Energy costs are cut in half in this design; the lighting load is a mere 2 watts.

Energy-conscious environment is a growing concern for the professional architect and designer. The American Institute of Architects (AIA) through most of its state and regional chapters, made "Design for the '80s" the main topic for all its conferences. In turn, city planners and architectural review boards are paying much more attention to conservation and alternate energy sources. The student whose goal is the building industry is well advised to select his or her school and instructors from among those who think AT.

Another American industry in dire need of change is automobile design and manufacturing. We all know the root problem: a dependency on imported oil to run inefficient cars produced by obsolete methods in an environment of confusion. High-gas-mileage imports from Japan and Europe help bridge the transportation gap, but the American economy has been bruised badly, and money going overseas hasn't helped the balance of payments.

Obviously, something must be done, and quickly. Mass transit is one answer, but the cure is long-term, and the patient is acutely ill. Enter the entrepreneur, the person with something to sell, the one with an idea. Ideas are flourishing since the gas crunch. Some are good, some are questionable, some are downright bad. While a few theories may prove impractical and not feasible, others show exciting glimpses of the future.

Some are simple adaptations of existing techniques. Take the work a team of graduate students from Carnegie-

Mellon University showed off in a 6,400-mile cross-country jaunt recently. Mario Zoccoli and Krishna Murti fitted their 1977 Chevy Impala with about $250 worth of off-the-shelf equipment from Sears Roebuck and gained 40 percent fuel efficiency, raising their mileage to 32 miles per gallon from 16.

They used low-friction graphited oil, low-rolling-resistance tires; engine modifications included a humidifier on the carburetor and an electro-mechanical control system. One part used on this typical American family car was taken from a shop vacuum cleaner. Most were available in neighborhood hardware and plumbing-supply stores.

Hobby projects such as this will make little difference in solving the major problem, however. Some feel that the internal combustion engine itself is obsolete and that other traction modes are destined to replace it. Electric-powered automobiles have been popular in the past. During the early decades of the twentieth century many were seen on city streets. But they were slow and rather clumsily designed. Battery weight and cost proved too much, and the electric car gave way to the Model-T Ford, the Chevrolet, the Dodge, the Buick, plus several hundred other makes built in cities around the country.

But the electric car is far from dead, although it has been held in an automotive limbo for sixty years. A resurgence is apparent as technological breakthroughs in battery design may make it possible to mass-produce electric vehicles by 1985 or sooner. The weight and size of battery packs required to generate enough power to move a sizable car safely along the nation's highways has been the biggest drawback. In an attempt to alleviate the problem, battery designers have come up with concepts using different materials and chemicals other than the accepted lead-acid type to create electric energy. They are understandably closedmouthed about their inventions.

While one of these designers, Teck Research, Inc., of Vancouver, British Columbia, could not give specific answers at this time, the Teck battery is a lithium-molydenum disulfide system and is one of several lithium-based batteries currently under development. General Motors is reported to have autos with long-life battery packs capable of 100-mile recharge ranges. Hybrid designs, in which a small internal combustion engine works in tandem with an electric motor, have been perfected by such pioneers as Briggs and Stratton, a Milwaukee manufacturer of engines that have powered many lawn mowers and garden tractors.

Steam-powered cars were manufactured for a short time at the turn of the century, but the self-starter and reliability of the gasoline engine soon closed the future for steam. Only the late William Lear, a designer of jet planes, held the view that the era of steam was yet to come. He put over $18 million into designs for steam-powered vehicles, but at his death his concepts had yet to prove viable.

Solar-Hydrogen Development Company of Los Angeles has perfected a car fueled by hydrogen in the form of "liquid hydride" derived from water. This company claims to be able to convert a stock auto for less than $400, to run on liquid hydride.

No industry is as eligible for decentralization as the electric power system. Power grids that fan out from major generating sources, such as hydroelectric dams or nuclear plants, are always vulnerable. Blackouts that spread across many states and affect millions of lives can be triggered by a malfunction in a tiny replay switch. Acts of nature and criminal vandalism can cause untold disruption of service. It is not

**The Windmobile. The sports car of the future? The air foil arching over the cockpit produces the vehicle's thrust from winds.** (Photo courtesy Sun-Wind, Inc.)

appropriate for so many to be dependent on systems that are potentially deficient. In this field, entrepreneurs have come quickly to the front.

All agree that wind is an energy source virtually untapped. But much debate has taken place about the kind of wind generator most economically suited for general use. Early plans, made in the last decade, called for huge windmills on 350-foot towers with 150-foot-long rotor blades. These have been largely unused. The National Aviation and Space agency (NASA) has designed a similar turbine atop Howard's Knob, near the town of Boone, North Carolina. This 2,000-kilowatt generator, built by General Electric and Boeing at a cost of $5.8 million for the Department of Energy, sends electricity to fewer than five hundred Watauga County homes at a cost of between six cents and twelve cents a kilowatt hour. Blue Ridge Membership Corp., which services the community, can buy power for 1.8 cents per kwh. So it appears that the Boone wind generator is an expensive experiment that, while it proves the feasibility of wind-generated electricity, will not be competitive until conventional fuel costs become level with Boone prices.

State-of-the-art changes in windmill design are continuous as inventors and marketing experts leap to fill the void caused by ascending fossil-fuel costs. A new concept, helical wind turbines (HWT), became available in the spring of 1981. Mounted on shorter towers—40 to 100 feet, determined by site—HWT are highly innovative. The helical airfoil is a high-torque, high-solidity unit ideally suited for low to moderate wind characteristics. It certainly appears different from any you may have seen. Instead of two or three blades rotating on a horizontal axis, HWT employs four sets of two blades spaced in depth, indexed helically, and designed so that high wind conditions are counteracted by drag air from the lead prop, which controls the leading edges of the deeper sets of blades.

Small machines such as HWT's could be interspersed in neighborhoods, or "forested" along coastal or desert "wind farms," where winds are usually constant. For community use, extra kilowatts could be shunted into the power grid. Power gained from wind farms could be counted on as a steady, dependable resource.

The federal DOE is planning to install 125 wind machines across America before 1982, selecting sites with different climates and utility companies. California Gov. Jerry Brown's Office of Appropriate Technology is cooperating with DOE through the California Energy Commission. The first of what is optimistically hoped to be four thousand wind generators throughout California was hoisted in July, 1980, on the windswept farmlands east of Petaluma. The rotor has three blades, each 16½ feet long, giving a mill diameter of about 34 feet. At its peak generating speed, the windmill spins at about 130 revolutions a minute, according to its builders, Wind Power Systems of San Diego. A system of gears will increase the speed through the shaft to about 1,825 rpm.

Another California OAT project sees 30 windmills on the southern anchorage area of the Golden Gate Bridge in San Francisco. These generators would have blades 22 feet in diameter. The Golden Gate Bridge District estimates the $300,000 installation costs would be recouped in six years. From that time on, the bridge electric costs, which are now $5,000 per month, would be nil.

A new career opportunity has developed as governmental agencies and utility districts search for best wind conditions. "Wind prospectors" get as much as $2,000 per site as consultants. "The cost of prospecting for wind is minuscule compared to prospecting for oil," states a report filed by the California Energy Commission. They think the rewards are far greater. According to the report, electricity generated by oil priced at thirty-five dollars per barrel is six cents per kwh. If the state erects wind turbines that generate only 7,000 megawatts by the year 2000, it would save 50 million barrels of oil per year. To do this it will be necessary to site between 3,000 and 4,000 windmills at a cost of $10 billion.

But where should the wind machines be placed? The report points out several sites where wind blows hard and long —in some cases too fiercely for use as future residential sites— that potentially could supply power equivalent to fifty Rancho Seco nuclear plants.

As a wind-potential example, the California Energy Commission report names San Gregorio Pass near Palm Springs where average wind speeds are greater than 20 miles per hour. This site alone could generate enough electricity to power 3 million homes. Other places where wind is strong and constant include the Warner Mountain Range of Modoc County in the Sierra Nevadas; dozens of spots in the Death Valley and Mohave Desert regions; passes in the Tehachapi Mountains in Kern County, north of Los Angeles; the Carquinez Strait, where the Sacramento-San Joaquin watershed empties into San Francisco Bay; and hundreds of places along California's north coast.

Add to these the thousands of mountainous terrains from east to west where the wind howls free and the potential for wind prospecting seems endless. Shorter power lines, a dependable power source, and pollution-free, safe energy is the reward for industrialists to throw their investments into the wind. Appropriate technology activists feel that when these three industries—building, automotive, and electrical power—decide to modify and decentralize, tensions will lessen in the United States, and new directions will be taken by other industries in this small world.

FOR YOU TO DO NOW:

Consult your local library for information on how to build a windmill. If you can build a small one, harness it to a used automobile generator; charge a storage battery, and see if you can produce the electricity to light a household lamp.

JOB OPPORTUNITIES:

Solar builder, automobile designer, mechanical engineer, wind prospector: AT thinkers will be in demand.

# CHAPTER 9

# AT IN AGRICULTURE



THE TWENTIETH century in America and other advanced nations saw a big shift from an agrarian to an industrial economy. Man's future seemed to be tied to big machines. Mammoth industries flourished, multinational corporations proliferated, and communications links interlaced the globe and the stratosphere. Indeed, the world was becoming smaller.

Satellite camera views, taken with infrared and heat-seeking lenses, showed agricultural lands depleting as the cities grew. Global temperature shifts affected rainfall, and desert regions spread over tropic areas. In the year 1979, farm production in the United States set new records—but not enough to offset declines in the rest of the world. Measured on a per capita basis, food production declined 3.3 percent, indicating that population increases continued to put pressure on the global warehouse.

North American farmland, particularly in the United States, shrank after the Second World War. In the decades of the '60s and '70s, the steady outward growth of city limits cut more and more deeply into arable farmland under production. Despite addition of several thousands of acres made available through aqueduct expansion in the Westlands district of central California, and the projected irrigation plans for Arizona along the Colorado River, western farmlands will continue to decrease as we approach the end of this century.

California heads the list of states which expect to lose productive acres in the '80s. As environmentalist movements fight to protect the remaining farmlands, their most strident opponents are the developers and their vocal lobbyists. However, a silent foe has been creeping up on the verdant California fields. It is erosion—by wind and water, compaction and pollution.

Priscilla C. Grew, director of the California state Department of Conservation, in what she admitted was a pessimistic report to the state Department of Food and Agriculture, said the state's 101 million acres were being eroded away faster than 1 inch every twenty-five years. Sound infinitesimal? Not when you realize that the natural rate of topsoil production is 1 inch every two thousand years—and you discover that California topsoils range in thickness from several feet to only a few inches.

The problem is man-induced and worldwide: overgrazing, road and highway construction, timber harvesting without replanting, extreme compaction with heavy equipment, nonorganic petrofertilization, the expanded use of off-road recreational vehicles.

When a roadbed is laid for freeways, the natural cover is disturbed and casual rains become gully washers. When trees are cut down, the natural watershed factors are eliminated and winds and rains quickly wash remaining topsoil into streams. Heavy semi-trailer produce trucks and farm tractors compact soft topsoil. As it dries and hardens, winds whip away tiny layer after layer, until all the soil has been scoured away to hardpan or bedrock. Trail bikes and jeeps and pickup trucks carve deep ruts into the hillsides and on so-called "unimproved" desert and prairie landscapes. Wind blows away the fragile veneer of topsoil because the tiny root structures have been crushed and can no longer hold the land together.

The delicate desert repairs itself so slowly that trails made by western settlers almost 150 years ago are still visible; thoughtless vandals of today are leaving their marks for posterity. There is no fast way to heal these wounds. Other damage that will heal more slowly is caused by overirrigating, which raises toxic salts from substrata that turn productive land into poisoned alkali flats.

Overgrazing can denude a pasture more quickly than the worst of nature's calamities—a lightning-induced prairie fire, for example. Pasturelands come back miraculously following range fires. But once roots have been chewed out and the pasture eroded, nothing can save the land for future use. "Study how a society uses its land," wrote E. F. Schumacher, "and you will come to some pretty reliable conclusions as to what its future will be."

To save the land from its predators, land-use planning has become a remedy appropriate to the times. Land-use planning determines growth of cities, placement of highways, densities of populations, and establishes open-space criteria. Congress and state legislatures have long refused to take a stand on land uses, relegating the unpleasant task to county and city planning commissions.

But the time has obviously come, and a federal inter-agency national agricultural lands study has been formulated over an eighteen-month period. The results are due on the President's desk sometime in 1981, and they will contain enough fuel to keep congressional fires burning for the next decade.

The arguments against any governmental regulation from Washington are well known. Developers, speculators, and their lobbies are well rehearsed in their cries about property rights and devaluation through land-use laws. AT activists feel it must be clear to anyone who reads the literature that land is no longer a private commodity, but is instead a national and global resource. It is from this perspective that they approach the future of appropriate technologies in agriculture.

Land, as a basis of all life, needs responsible care and nurturing. National Lands for People (NLP), an organization of small-farm agriculturists, claims this kind of nurturing and care can come only from the small farmers. NLP has its headquarters in Fresno, California, the heart of bountiful San Joaquin Valley. Small farms in the San Joaquin can be 160-acre homesteads or 1,280-acre family-corporation farms.

The Reclamation Act passed by Congress in 1902 governs irrigation water flowing through Reclamation Bureau pumps to San Joaquin Valley farms. The law restricts land holdings for users to 160 acres per adult family member. Thus a family of four could legally irrigate only 320 acres with Reclamation water. Further, the law says the family must live on or near the land it irrigates. Yet farms of several thousand acres owned by agribusiness combines, with no resident farmers, are not uncommon in the San Joaquin, and are the rule in Imperial Valley near the Mexican border.

The major oil companies, who are the resource for the petrofertilizers and petrochemicals used widely on the large farms, have large agribusiness holdings. They include Chevron, Shell, Union, Mobil, Tenneco, and Getty, among others. The Southern Pacific Railroad, which is the largest private landowner in California and several western states, manages gargantuan farms throughout the area. SP was granted land when it built its railroad. The land was to have been subdivided among the settlers after the railroad was finished. SP held tightly to its property rights, and according to NLP, breaks the law two ways: by using water it is not entitled to, and by hoarding land in the first place.

Small farmers feel they have a better control over the tools of destruction that big agribusiness misuse. They say crop selection, fertilization, and irrigation can all be handled better on small farms. And they maintain stoutly that small farms do pay off financially and productively. Agribusiness farmers say they can produce more goods per acre through modernization in equipment and methods. Small farmers reply that they can be more efficient because of their size—because they waste less, their methods are better for the land in the long run.

A 1980 report from the U. S. Department of Agriculture

warns that fifty of the largest food-manufacturing firms in America will completely control farm products by the year 2000 if they continue the upward climb started in 1950. Food-market economists have two views, each favoring its own perception. One—the specialists who work for supermarket chains who own land, grow, package, and distribute their own products—claim they can get food to the family dinner table cheaper than going through middlemen. The second—independent growers, cooperatives, and jobbers—claim that the supermarket approach is a quick way to monopoly in the food chain and higher prices in the final analysis.

NLP brings up another point: the Reclamation Act of 1902, requiring owners to live on or near the property they farm, set up a plan for settling the countryside with homes and rural centers. This offers a sense of community which is healthier for the people as well as the land. They give the small city of Sanger as an example.

Sanger, population 11,250 in 1980, is a town surrounded by family-owned farms. It has schools and shops, churches and parks. It is the hub of social activities twelve months of the year. Its streets are clean and tree lined; its residents live in single-family dwellings and are a well-knit community.

In contrast, NLP takes you down one of the arrow-straight country roads that crisscross Westlands in north-south grid lines laid out a century ago by federal survey teams. As far as the eye can see are thousands of acres of cotton, or barley, or potatoes. No forests cool the landscape; there are no parks or settlements of homes; no evidence of community can be seen. The shimmering heat waves and the unwavering blacktop road are broken only by irrigation ditches and an occasional worker's pickup truck. Far away a tractor raises a cloud of dust that is picked up by a vagrant wind; small cyclones of rising air build and spin over the land. That and the gray-green crop are all you see until you come to a small crossroads collection of structures in bad repair: a gasoline station, half a dozen shacks, three bars, a small grocery store, few people. Black and Mexican farm workers stop for supplies or a cold beer. The heat is oppressive. The scene is depressing. It is not a place to tarry long.

NLP would like to transform this intersection. They visualize the agribusiness spreads broken down to family-size plots with homes on them. They see trees as wind-breaks. They would like more thriving communities like Sanger with parks and schools and churches where migrant workers can settle down and raise their families. They see more diversified farming activities, the kinds of crops more in tune with the '80s and '90s. They would not use the pesticides favored by agribusiness, nor such great quantities of petro-fertilizers. They feel they would be much better stewards of the land than corporate heads sitting in New York, Hong Kong, or Amsterdam.

Small-farm stewardship would be aided by researchers who promote alternatives for chemical pesticides. Integrated pest management (IPM) is a complex process incorporating a multitude of cultural and biological practices to defeat pest infestations. As few pesticides as possible are used in IPM programs.

Almost a century ago, in 1888, the U. S. Department of Agriculture entomologists discovered that vedalia beetles from Australia were natural enemies to "cottony cushion," a scale that threatened the California citrus industry. Within a decade, the beetle virtually eliminated the scale, saving millions of dollars for growers. Fifty years of this natural and highly appropriate method of control came abruptly to an end after World War II, when DDT was introduced to the citrus groves. DDT killed all the "bad" beetles, and it killed all the good insects—including the vedalia beetle—at the same time.

Worldwide, introduction of natural pest enemies of some 186 "bad" bugs has achieved a degree of control. Nearly four hundred successful programs in biological pest control have recently been tabulated by scientists. Agribusiness farmers are reluctant to give up their chemical "insurance" for natural methods which are necessarily experimental and constantly in flux. Small farmers, because of their close relationship with the land they plant and live upon, seem more willing to put the extra effort into producing and protecting their crops.

Natural pest control successes are evident across the United States, as well as in Central and South America. This is good news to the workers who must spend time in the fields. Farm workers have taken a personal interest in natural pest control since DDT was found to be toxic, and DBCP, the controversial soil fumigant used to combat nematodes, was identified as a mutagen and carcinogen. Occupational hazards from handling parathion, an all-purpose pesticide, include residue poisoning. Human sperm formation is listed as a "non-target" recipient of pesticide overuse, which means the poison was not aimed at the danger area, but got there just the same.

Natural soil fertilization can be as successful as natural pest control, and the practice can convert large as well as small farms away from petrochemical fertilizers. Wehah Farms, a family corporation with 3,000 acres in rice near Richvale, California, grows a portion of their product organically. The corporation includes four Lundberg brothers—

Wendell, Eldon, Harlan, and Homer. Their late father, Albert, established the farm.

No chemicals of any kind are used in Wehah's organic fields, which have been certified by the California Certified Organic Farmers association. Clover, oats, and purple vetch are mixed with rice straw and husks to build up humus and organic matter that feeds the rice plantings. Their location, at the head end of a canal system direct from the pure Feather River, insures no chemical irrigation runoff from upstream farms. Mosquito fish help control insects.

Organic cultural practices are admittedly expensive. But the bottom-line price may be lower when all costs are considered. Farm-oriented appropriate technology is making long and steady strides. Examples abound:

Department of Agriculture Secretary Bob Bergland introduced in 1980 a low-cost, portable solar unit designed specifically to warm farm homes, dry grain, or heat pig sties and chicken houses. The units, on which DOA holds the patents, are manufactured and distributed by small companies. Plans are available for do-it-yourself farmers. The kits cost around $2,500. Units were tested under varying conditions in Quincy, Illinois; Guthrie, Oklahoma; Bismarck, North Dakota; Los Lunas, New Mexico; Culpepper, Virginia; and Fryeburg, Maine.

Milk cows in an Oregon university barn are being washed down with water heated on rooftop solar collectors. In addition, heat transfer by milk is accomplished. Milk must be cooled from the 100-degree temperature at which it leaves the cow to a 40-degree holding temperature. The milk heat is transferred to water, which in turn is used for cleaning the cows and the barns.

The first privately owned solar dairy in the country was owned by Ted Dykzeul, of Oakdale, California. In operation since 1977, the rooftop collector cost $5,000. On hot summer days the sun-heated water is so hot it must be cooled to washing temperature around 120 degrees. In the coldest of winter, the water temperature will be 90 degrees.

With the rise of OPEC oil prices, and the falling domestic petroleum production, farmers are filling a need by producing crops for ethanol and methanol distillation and digestion. Whether used in combination with gasoline to form gasohol, or used straight, the mid-1980s goal of 500 million gallons set by the Department of Energy calls for the number of alcohol distilleries to grow tenfold almost immediately.

To answer that need, Archer-Daniels-Midland Company of Decatur, Illinois, announced in May, 1980, its plans to boost its capacity 400 percent before the end of 1981. Archer-Daniels, the nation's largest alcohol producer for automotive power, makes 54 million gallons a year at its Decatur plant. Additional plant facilities in Peoria, where it is buying Hiram Walker & Sons distillery, and in Cedar Rapids, Iowa, where it is building a new plant, will raise its total production in 1981 to 260 million gallons annually.

Gasohol buyers in Iowa and Nebraska receive a discount on gasoline taxes, and a summertime estimate in 1980 showed over 2,000 of the nation's 175,000 service stations selling it. With the increasing popularity of gasohol, the need for grains becomes paramount. To satisfy this need, DOE earmarked 5 million tons of corn originally destined for the Soviet Union. Embargoes on other grain exports are expected to supply sufficient grain to keep all American distilleries working round-the-clock shifts.

The moral question still has not been answered, however. AT people point to other products available from the farming sector for alcohol conversion, and for new oil sources: alcohol from wood chips, forest gleanings, and urban waste, as Chuck Stone has shown; energy from more than one thousand replantable shrubs and trees, some of them potential oil producers.

Dr. Melvin Calvin, Nobel Prize-winning chemist from the University of California, Berkeley, feels "plant petroleum" would be cheaper to produce than fossil petroleum, and the stranglehold on American industry by OPEC could be broken if oil is grown freely as crops. Dr. Calvin envisions "gasoline trees"—the plant species *euphorbia*—which produce a latex that can be processed to yield hydrocarbons with the same capacity for energy as fossil fuels.

Dr. Calvin hopes that continuing research might produce strains of *euphorbia* which would yield 30 barrels of oil per acre. He estimates one acre of land can support 43,500 *euphorbia* plants and yield 10 barrels of oil under present conditions. Harvest and refining costs run about $150 per acre; this would place the "barrel head" cost of *euphorbia* oil at $15 per barrel, which is far less than domestic or imported oil prices.

As more of this kind of photosynthetic oil is produced, the price would go down still farther, according to Dr. Calvin. He says at least 10 percent of national requirements could be met within a period of five years if a program was started now. As an added incentive, the plants would also yield about 15 tons of firewood per acre every year.

The tasty sunflower seed has been successfully made into diesel oil, which is a necessity for running large farm tractors. But the sunflower seed seems inconsequential when compared with an oil pump.

The most exciting plant to grab the notice of energy-conscious American agriculturists is an obscure desert bush called jojoba (pronounced hoHOba). Jojoba could replace petroleum, if statistics are credible. The fact is, however, that the "oil" extracted from this humble plant is not an oil at all—it is a wax. It can be hydrogenated into a solid wax, second only to carnauba in hardness. Or it can be sulfurized into a motor oil that seldom needs changing.

The pure oil, when filtered, is the finest-grade lubricant ever known, surpassing even sperm whale oil, which has been banned from the United States under the protection of the Endangered Species Act of 1971. Other uses for jojoba oil are as a base for penicillin, shampoo, moisturizing cream (it never becomes rancid), salad dressing, and a cure for acne.

Known by the chemical industry for decades, jojoba had never been agriculturally produced until 1976, when 300 acres were planted. The goal for Jojoba International, a small group that is promoting the product, is 1 million acres; about 5,000 acres were planted by 1981. Climate is the only enemy of jojoba. While it can endure extreme desert heat, temperatures under 20 degrees will kill off buds. So it will be planted mostly in the southwest desert lowlands of New Mexico, Arizona, and California.

Waste vegetation on farms is another small gold mine. Sweet sorghum and sugarcane stalks, maize stalks, rice straw, field crop straw from barley, wheat, and oats—in fact any cellulose fiber can be processed to make alcohol. Tons of vegetables are rejected from packing sheds daily. Mangels (large and coarse sugar beets), buffalo gourds, yams, cassavas—all are high-starch, high-sugar plants. Carloads of melons are rejected in the field and left to rot. Artichokes—small, overripe, frost damaged—are discarded. One small campus project at the University of California at Davis hopes to produce 400,000 gallons of alcohol a year utilizing just such rejects.

Some people are skeptical about alcohol and gasohol. They point out that alcohol production is energy intensive, that it costs too much in energy to produce a trade-off. Secretary of Agriculture Bob Bergland feels that the uncertainty of corn crops would make dependence on that commodity as risky as dependence on any other source. Nevertheless, those who make, sell, and use alcohol are enthusiastic about its potential. They look to agriculture as the main source for biomass, the vegetable "ore" of the future.

Other agricultural energy sources are being studied extensively. The general viewpoint is that alternative power sources are subject only to geography, the time element, and the climate.

Not the least of energy opportunities is small-scale hydroelectric development. Students of water resources estimate that tens of thousands of megawatts can be generated annually by rural residents living near small creeks, rivers, waterfalls, or rapids. Even irrigation canals that have water drops (small dams or weirs) offer power potential.

David C. Willer, manager of water resource projects for Tudor Engineering, a San Francisco-based firm, says it is financially practical to install generators, some producing 5 kwh, which come in a package that need only be placed in a running stream to provide enough power for most homes and farms.

Farm land not up to "prime" category can be used to plant fast-growing oak and eucalyptus groves for firewood. Desert ranches can grow mesquite as a fuel crop. Mesquite can also be used as a cattle-feed supplement. Farmers in southern states who have always dreaded the fast-growing water hyacinth can now breathe more easily: this once monstrous lily, it has been discovered, is a fine source for methane and methanol. The water hyacinth doubles its size every day in a pond or slow-running stream. As a cash crop it no longer need be feared.

Another pest vine that has plagued southern farmers is known as kudzu. It was first introduced into the United States from Japan in 1876 as an ornamental plant. Soon this rapidly expanding vine covered trees, utility poles, and agricultural land. Now researchers are developing a process to extract methane through bacterial digestion of the plant, which can grow over a foot a day and can be farmed on soil not suitable for other cash crops.

Surplus potatoes in northwestern fields can be put to use for their high-starch value in alcohol production. Farmer Ron Miller of Alfalfa, Oregon, brews his own in his home laundry room. "I'm not interested in gasohol," he will tell you. "Cars and tractors can run just as well on pure alcohol." Miller's annual gasoline bill has been as high as $3,500. Now he is turning part of his potato crop into enough alcohol to run his farm machinery and trucks. With Miller, it is a matter of survival.

Not all synthetics are viewed negatively by AT people. To increase yields, the USDA research laboratory at Peoria, Illinois, has developed a "super-slurper," a foamy combination of synthetic compounds that makes soil and seeds more absorbent. Corn and sorghum yields have increased from 10 to 49 percent after application of super-slurper. Fifty cents' worth of super-slurper used on cotton seed returned fifty dollars' worth of increased yields in a Texas test, according to USDA reports.

With such adjuncts as super-slurper, greater use of marginal lands, smaller farms, by-product utilization, organic methods, and small-stream hydroelectric generation, agriculture will provide a vitality to this small world. More career-oriented farmers and innovators will be needed as these changes take place.


FOR YOU TO DO NOW:

Try to spend some time on a farm—preferably an organic one—or visit a farming community. See how the farmer utilizes natural methods of fertilization, selects his crop for appropriate uses, rotates his seeding schedule. Consult books and agricultural pamphlets to learn about composting, intensive farming, "green manure," sheet mulching.


JOB OPPORTUNITIES:

Agricultural economist, farmer, grain miller, biologist, plant pathologist, field hand, tool designer, machinist: these are only a few of the jobs for AT ag people.

# CHAPTER 10
# AT IN FORESTRY

*PLANTING TREES TAKES . . .*
*THE ABILITY TO SING UNDER*
*ALL SORTS OF SITUATIONS.*

HUNTER SHELDON
THE TREE PEOPLE MEMBER

IF YOU are concerned about agricultural land depletion in this small world, consider the forests. The word used in United Nations' studies on the earth's bald spots is "desertification." Millions of acres are made barren by encroaching civilization.

All around the globe the picture is repeated: trees disappear; remaining land is farmed poorly, overgrazed, windwashed, and finally it is desert—nonproductive. The American version differs only in geography and in a determined effort by AT people to "do something about it."

As the United States frontier moved slowly westward,

the forests were cut down at a steady rate. New England, by 1850, had 80 percent of its land cleared for farming. West Coast logging operations between 1850 and 1970 were almost completely uncontrolled. Water resources, commercial and sports fisheries, and recreational facilities all suffered the results of clear-cutting forestlands. Sediment muddied clear streams, destroyed fish spawning grounds, and killed the inland fishing industry. Once-verdant coastal hillsides became snag-filled brushlands. Logging towns flourished, then died, leaving ghost towns.

Forestry practices are changing. The forest as our forebears knew it may return. That is if the same AT stewardship needed on farmlands is carried on in the woodlands. Some of the good changes may have come about because of the problems in city life. Wealthy people able to retreat to the hillsides of upstate New York and to the rural woods of Connecticut and Rhode Island—the gentleman farmers—have influenced the decline of land clearing in New England. The total number of acres cleared for farming has lessened measurably, and the land planted in forest has increased.

In the Yankee Forest, as those wooded mountains and valleys in New England are known, the wilderness has nearly been reestablished. If these newborn New England forestlands were efficiently managed, say conservationists, new appropriate technologies could emerge. New economies could be sustained.

A report by Yale University researchers says that as many as 60,000 new jobs could be provided by a resurging forestry industry. However, the report continues, all of the Yankee Forest could become another wasteland unless proper management controls are introduced.

The tourist industry could suffer. Enticed by the natural beauty of the winding roads and rolling hillsides that in the spring are alive with flowering dogwood and other blooms, or by the blaze of frost-limned autumnal leaves, people come to New England from all over the United States and Europe at these special times of the year. Should inappropriate methods be used to maintain the forests, to harvest the wood, to remove deadfalls and clear the underbrush, a multimillion-dollar industry could die.

The rising cost of petrofuels is giving impetus to a movement to cut the trees in the Yankee Forest. Proper management is a must, conservationists say. Much of the forested land in New York State—85 percent—is owned by people whose average holding is 40 acres. In Connecticut and Rhode Island, however, 85 percent of the forest is owned by those whose parcel size is closer to 10 acres. Without a clear line of communications between these communities, the thought of orderly harvest seems unlikely. But with new management concepts it is not an impossibility.

Some bright lights are on the horizon. A bond issue, for instance, in Burlington, Vermont, was passed by voters, making possible the construction of a municipal power plant fueled by wood chips. And in New Hampshire new legislation has been prepared to modernize the forestry policy. It would concentrate on clearing the woods economically and ecologically.

It is not only the Yankee Forest that needs dedicated leadership in forestry. Few conferences have been held in governmental circles to develop guidelines. The Pennsylvania woodlands, the mountains of Tennessee, the Carolinas, and Ohio are filled with millions of tons of wood to be harvested wisely and turned into power, or processed for paper, particle board, and other pulp products.

Forest debris can be fuel for unwanted fires or for energy. Broken branches, deadfalls, old and dying trees should all be removed. Miscellaneous branches and pieces can be converted to chips for vermiculture (composting for worm beds), pyrolized for steam power, or digested for alcohol. Hardwoods can be transformed into charcoal. All forest fibers can be composted for garden and farm fertilizers. Nothing need be wasted. Fire danger could be lessened.

"In its resurgence, wood will set an example of the optimum energy solution," wrote David A. Tillman in *Wood as an Energy Resource*. Tillman thinks that deriving energy from many fuels that supply modest amounts is more stable than relying on only one source, such as oil and later, nuclear power. From the cataclysmic effect of war or political anomalies, the effect of supply cutoffs would be disastrous to an economy and a nation. Because wood is one of the truly renewable resources, it can be kept in adequate supply quite easily, in all sections of the country, and even in cities, if it is properly managed.

We think of forests as remote places where someday we might chance to vacation. We think in terms of Alaskan wilds and Washington rain forests, of Upper Michigan woodlands along Lake Superior, and the Okefenokee Swamp in southern Georgia and northern Florida. We seldom think of every city as a forest.

Modern cities can be harsh, huge, dirty, alienating. That is the reason trees belong there. "Trees are a putting down of roots, a dance into air," says a booklet put out by the California Department of Forestry. Titled *The Hip-Pocket Urban Tree Planter*, the booklet encourages urban forestry in an enchanting manner.

"City trees make our urban neighborhoods more livable. Trees create a buffer from the often frantic pace of urban life; they aid in cooling our homes, provide a habitat for urban wildlife, and absorb noise, pollutants, and unpleasant odors." These are the words of Huey D. Johnson, California Secretary of Resources, in a foreword to the booklet.

"Bringing the trees back to our inner cities," Johnson continues, "is a challenge for getting neighbors together, for community self-help programs. By softening our concrete and asphalt with greenery, city trees remind us all that our natural resources are the basis of our survival."

The manual is designed to help people respond to the challenge of restoring the fast-dwindling urban tree resource despite reduced government spending. It shows how one can begin to "see" the urban forest that grows in backyards, on rooftops in containers, on decks and fire escapes. "Once you sta:t seeing this urban forest," says the booklet, "you'll probably feel slightly different about where you live—greener, fresher, better grounded. You'll probably want to plant some trees."

City trees release oxygen and absorb carbon dioxide, freshening city air. They help settle dust, block winds, buffer noise, screen harsh buildings, and add to city and neighborhood pride. Trees also increase property values and expand employment opportunities in landscape contracting and maintenance. But they cost money to plant.

Fortunately, there are many ways to raise the money that makes tree planting possible. These include old-fashioned fund-raising; demonstration planting by a special-interest group like a utility company or water district; tree donor programs; labor-swapping programs (matching each donation with a pledge of labor worth the cost of a tree). Large corporate sponsors will usually find a tree planting well worth the cost of advertising. Tax-deductible charitable contributions can be solicited for planting trees.

The fact that neighborhood people care about having trees planted is the key to the success of the Oakland, California, Tree Task Force. They have planted on park land, school grounds, along freeways, and up and down Oakland's streets, with no cost to the city or the taxpayer. Most of the money is supplied through a nonprofit "Adopt-a-Block" program.

"Where the city's 'we'll-do-everything-for-you' approach has resulted in thousands of vandalized trees, the Task Force has lost only a couple of trees," they proudly proclaim. "And that was done by one person on one night. We went back and talked to him. He replaced the trees he had damaged, and now he waters and takes care of every tree on the street."

Another group is called the Tree People. This is also a nonprofit organization, one founded on a dream by fifteen-year-old Andy Lipkis, who noticed the trees around his summer camp in the mountains east of Los Angeles were dying of smog poisoning.

Andy spent three years, on and off, trying and failing to get smog-resistant trees planted to replace the ones that were dying. He finally convinced twenty camps to participate in a reforestation program. But he still needed the trees. He asked the California Department of Forestry for twenty thousand seedlings, but CDF said the trees would cost $600.

Andy then approached the Los Angeles *Times*, which published a page-one account of his struggle. Within three weeks, Andy had received $10,000 to help put trees in the ground, mostly in fifty-cent donations from *Times* readers. Thus began the Tree People, which is now thriving as a truly citizen-based group. Andy now remarks, "It seems like most activities are really about people getting together."

Trees can be used for beauty, for the fruit they offer, or for the valuable wood that can be harvested. One of the fine hardwoods that is easily grown in American cities as well as in the country is the black walnut. These hardy trees, native to the midwestern states along the Ohio and Mississippi valleys, were all but wiped out when the railroad was laid during the last part of the nineteenth century. Burned for fuel on steam locomotives, cut for railroad ties and right-of-way fences, long-lasting walnut logs were favorites along the line.

In the years following World War II, diminishing supplies of all hardwoods led to the practice of "printing" wood grains on other materials to simulate hardwood; polyurethane, a petroplastic, is used for many so-called "pecan" or other wood finishes. The few good logs produced in America were shipped to Japan or Europe. In return, cabinet shops in the United States were forced to purchase their plywoods and "flitch stock" (fancy veneers used in fine furniture) from overseas suppliers.

The Fine Hardwoods Association and the American Forest Products Industries have been making strong efforts toward seeding and planting domestic hardwood forests. Because black walnut can be readily hybridized for fast growth, it can be harvested within a relatively short investment time. Luther Burbank's "Paradox" hybrids grew 80 feet tall and 2 feet in diameter in fourteen years.

Hybrid walnuts do not need the deep loam soil of their native forebears. They grow especially well on sites that are well-drained where annual rainfall totals 15 inches. The black walnut is highly favored among candymakers for its distinctive flavor. The tree is the root stock for the softer-shelled English or Persian walnut grown successfully throughout California.

Some city planners look at hybrid black walnut trees as a recyclable tree for use in park lands, on golf courses and along city streets. The nut crop and the wood, harvested and sold, would pay for other plantings. Wood from one mature walnut tree would sell for as much as $30,000 on the 1980 market. The annual nut crop is worth from $50 to $100 per tree.

However, care for black walnut trees is very important. If there is any evidence of nails, barbed wire, or clothesline hooks having been imbedded in the trunks, their value goes to zero. Metal objects ruin expensive veneer saws; the hardwood sawmill will not accept the logs.

Hulls from nut crops have a high food value as well. The nutritional value of hulls after being ground up and used as a supplemental feed for dairy animals includes protein and as much as 28 percent carbohydrates. Surplus hulls are also used for manufacturing charcoal briquets, the kind widely used for barbecues.

Diamond/Sunsweet, Inc., a large fruit and nut processing company, has built in Stockton, California, a huge plant whose total energy supply will come from walnut shells and a co-generation process. Construction cost is $3.5 million, which while it may sound high, is less than the cost for cleaning up after the Three Mile Island accident. Diamond/Sunsweet expects to have a surplus of energy to sell to the local utility company.

Front-yard forestry may have another use that is very appropriate. Leaves from the mulberry tree are the only food eaten by the most exotic worm of all: the silkworm. The technology of breeding silkworms and spinning silk is enchanting. We were pleasantly surprised and fascinated when we met Nancy Simpson, whose hobby is sericulture—the production of silk from egg to fiber.

Few attempts have been made to raise silkworms in America. Racial, political, and natural barriers have successfully kept this industry from developing in the United States. Nancy Simpson has no desire to start a cottage industry in her Sacramento home. But she has everything needed to begin such an operation. She has the eggs—*Bombyx mor*—which are imported through southern California and Texas sources. She keeps them in her refrigerator until spring, when food will be available for the tiny worms that will be hatched. And she has the food.

Silkworms live only on mulberry leaves, and Sacramento abounds in mulberry trees. Once hatched, the worms eat voraciously, day and night. They set up a din that Nancy Simpson compares with rain falling on a tin roof. In four weeks they grow ten thousand times their original weight. They grow from tiny specks to fat worms the size of a finger. Then they seek a place to spin their cocoons.

Mrs. Simpson supplies twigs, egg cartons, cardboard boxes, and other varied environments for the cocoon making. It seems the silkworms are not really choosy. The cocoons are of long strands of silk that unbroken can stretch as far as a half mile. As they spin, the worms shrink to chrysalis stage, giving up legs and form until the metamorphosis has been completed. Just before that stage is reached, the cocoon is oven baked, then simmered in boiling water. This last process softens the rigid skin, removing the serucin, a waxy substance that hardens and protects the cocoon.

Once the cocoons are pliable, they can be stored until

the spinning process begins. Twenty-five cocoons equal one spool of silk thread, to be woven into a finished product—a fine blouse, a nubby skirt, drapery. As we watched Nancy Simpson spin a spool of thread, we had the thought—what a great technology for some ambitious entrepreneur to begin: the new American silk industry.

And the energy cost is nil!

With unemployment a chronic problem in inner cities, additional tree-related jobs and careers are possible.

An expanding nursery and landscape contracting industry is one result of vigorous urban forestry efforts. Tree-maintenance services may be a small-business solution to cutbacks in city tree maintenance crews.

Woodworking crafts provide a ready market for the walnut, apple, and other fine wood that may be wasted where urban development has taken over orchard lands.

Firewood is a commodity with an expanding market as more people change to fireplaces for domestic heat. Wood comes into its own when crackling merrily in a fireplace or burning slowly in a controlled-heat woodstove.

Ken Smith, former design team manager for the California OAT and more recently head of the state energy commission, has designed what he claims is "the ultimate" in fireplaces. In the Smith energy-efficient fireplace, hot air is circulated through an insulated rock heat-storage bed. Stored heat is then channeled through a conventional furnace vent system. Richard Hill, at the University of Maine, has developed and tested a similar prototype.

If wood is the most economical fuel, it can double its value by heating water in cold, sunless winter months. So thinks Bill Hollibaugh, Petaluma, California, entrepreneur.

The simple wood stove takes an important place among more exotic forms of alternatives at energy shows. All manufacturers and distributors of low-tech energy units need representatives to demonstrate and sell their products.

His brainchild is the Holly Hydro Heater, a "water jacket" that is placed inside any woodstove or fireplace. Hooked up to household plumbing and the home hot-water tank and other auxiliary storage tanks, sufficient hot water can be collected to use in tubs and room radiators. A small woodstove can heat hundreds of gallons of water that flows through the Holly Hydro Heater. As long as there is a fire burning, hot water is available.

Cost of firewood may be high on wood lots. Green-cut and dried white oak can be as much as $180 per cord (1981 prices). The heat value per cord is 28 million Btu's (British thermal units). This would equal 154 gallons of No. 2 fuel oil, 19 cubic feet of natural gas, or a little more than 4,100 kwh of electricity. The price of the last three will dictate whether purchased oak fireplace wood is economical.

For those fortunate enough to live near public forests, the wood is free. Forest service experts estimate a minimum of 500 million dry tons of residue wood—windfalls, logging tailings—in public and private forests. The woods were closed to scavengers until 1973 when they were opened to non-commercial wood gatherers. Free permits are available at U.S. Forest Service offices.

This information may lead you to the forest, where a new career may be awaiting you, as it was for Jim and Pauline Holland. Jim Holland was an electrical engineer, his wife a telephone switchboard operator. Today they live in the forests of the Sierra Nevada and operate a "mobile sawmill." The Hollands contract to remove and cut to size dead or dying trees often found on private property. They earn about $150 for every 1,000 board feet they cut.

According to Jim Holland, he can expect almost 1,000 board feet from a log 16 feet long and 3 feet in diameter. The woods are filled with that size log, going to waste. Jim and Pauline and their portable sawmill should be able to keep well occupied for some time to come. Theirs is a highly appropriate technology.

Latest research from the U. C. Berkeley Lawrence Laboratory shows that first-class crude oil can be made from soft wood fibers (pine, fir, spruce, redwood, etc.) as well as from other vegetable fibers. Dr. Sabri Ergun, a physicist, has led a team that has developed the technology and engineering. According to Dr. Ergun, oil can be produced at one-third the cost of making alcohol from wood chips. He adds that only 40 percent of wood is suitable for making alcohol, while all wood is amenable to oil production.

Using Ergun's process, 5,000 tons of stock can produce 10,000 barrels of oil daily, and can be set up in any area where wood, municipal organic wastes, and agricultural residue are available. And that means everywhere.

It seems there are many career opportunities available within urban and rural forests, either planting and maintaining, or harvesting and processing. And the forest is the perfect place to practice appropriate technology.

FOR YOU TO DO NOW:

Visit your city tree-planting department. Inquire about planting a tree at your home or in your neighborhood, for beautification and energy. Start a tree-planting program in your school or neighborhood. Plant one tree yourself.

JOB OPPORTUNITIES:

Forester, lumberman, silvaculturist, park manager, sericulturist, weaver, physicist: all can "tell the AT forest from the trees."

# CHAPTER 11

# AT ON THE TRAIL

*. . . ALL YOU NEED TO LIVE A GOOD LIFE LIES ABOUT YOU.*

BILL MOLLISON
PERMACULTURE TWO, 1979

A NEW sensitivity has been nurtured through appropriate technology and its ideals: preservation of nature, protecting the wilderness, replanting trees, clearing streams, designing recreation sites, maintaining fisheries, fighting forest fires, constructing and bolstering flood levees, restoring bridges, stabilizing dunes, guarding the desert. An even dozen activities, all tied in with the out-of-doors, all trail oriented, all nature sensitive, and all very appropriate.

As America seeks different modes of recreation, natural resources suffer. Careless campers start forest fires; thoughtless drivers careen over beaches in dune buggies; off-road vehicles carve up a fragile desert. Acid rains born of urban factories fall on eastern mountains, lakes, and streams, killing fish and reptilian species. Every year the Petrified Forest in Arizona loses up to 12 tons of its main attraction: chip by chip and stone by stone, petrified wood is lost to thieving vandals. Offshore oil drilling threatens wildlife and the fishing industry, both sport and commercial. Developers take huge chunks of once-wild territory around remote mountain lakes for condominiums, ski runs, golf courses, parking lots and motel-hotel spaces.

All across the country harried park rangers, United States Forest Service workers, Bureau of Land Management employees, state agencies, sheriffs' deputies, and environmentalists wage an ongoing battle to save the wild scenes and improve them where possible. Sadly, many feel these are battles they are doomed to lose.

A case in point is what Mark Twain referred to as ". . . the fairest picture the whole earth affords"—Lake Tahoe, a lake of unsurpassed beauty that straddles the boundary between California and Nevada. In 1872, when Twain visited Tahoe, it was seldom seen by the casual visitor. Gold miners were busy working the Mother Lode, on the slopes of the Sierra Nevada 30 to 40 miles to the west. The great railroads were laid out at least 15 miles to the north, and transcontinental highways followed the railroad lines. Virtually few, other than hardy and seasoned hikers and campers, came to Tahoe in numbers before the 1920s. It was indeed off the beaten track.

The lake is large: 12 miles wide and 21 miles long. Fed by glacial streams and spring runoff from the surrounding snow-covered mountains, it is 1,500 feet deep and stands at 6,225 feet elevation. It is situated in a natural bowl, ringed by peaks that soar over 3,000 feet above. The depth and clarity of the water give it a breathtakingly blue color; it hits the visitor's eyes like a flash of cobalt in the sun, too blue to be real, when first it is glimpsed through the ponderosa pine forest.

But things have been happening to lovely Lake Tahoe, the "noble sheet of blue water" seen by Mark Twain. It has come upon bad days. Highways now surround its once fresh shore. Streets and homes climb the hills where just a few years ago only foot trails meandered. The south end is bristling with high-rise hotels and gambling establishments. Traffic is continuous, even with the gasoline shortage. The air, once clear and bracing, is tainted with exhaust fumes, particularly bad when there is a temperature inversion, which happens often.

The peaceful, woodsy scene has changed to blatant honky-tonk. Worst of all, the clear blue water is green with algae in the bays where development has caused erosion; the edges of the south end are scummed because too much sewage effluent has drained into its depths.

Dr. Charles Goldman, an internationally respected limnologist (a specialist in lakes) has told people worried about the future of Lake Tahoe, as well as other freshwater lakes that are being defiled, that it takes seven hundred years for a lake with Tahoe's proportions and flow to recycle. This decade's pollution will take until 2780 to be rectified naturally. Goldman, who has explored Tahoe's icy depths in a tiny submarine, says that unless governmental agencies take a comprehensive approach to the problem and stop development, erosion will kill the once-clear lake.

It is not easy for government to halt development, however. Political pressures are brought to bear. Some agencies, with the help of civic groups like the Sierra Club and environmental committees, are taking steps in that direction.

"Few built-up subdivisions have taken steps to halt erosion," says Carla Bard, chairwoman of the California Water Resources Control Board. Her agency has authority to protect the lake. However, thousands of lot owners will not be able to build on property worth some $200 million if Carla Bard fulfills her mandate. A $95 million program for erosion control will be needed. Taxpayers, developers, builders, and speculators all scream to the Sierra peaks about regulatory agencies and governmental "meddling."

Apparently few were thinking of the pristine beauty of Lake Tahoe when the land sellers moved in. The green pines, snow-covered peaks, blue water vistas—these were objects for postcards, for sales brochures. Someone else could worry about saving them later, if anyone gave them a thought at all.

Well, someone is thinking—about Lake Tahoe, the desert, the seashore, and all the wondrous places where people can become one with their surroundings: where quiet prevails; where fish run in fast, clear water; where a family can camp or hike in the beauty of nature. They are called AT activists. Unlike their counterparts on the Lower East Side of New York, their lives are spent in the wilderness, preparing trails and defending the forest.

Gary Fuller is a modern-day trailblazer. He works in the trackless wilderness of the Cleveland National Forest on the remote side of San Diego County in southern California. Much of his working day is spent alone.

Fuller's job is laying out hiking trails, working with contour maps in an effort to make the often steep terrain more easily passable. The tremendous growth in hiking as a recreational pastime has put major pressure on the Cleveland Forest's engineers, and experienced people like Gary Fuller with trail-building knowledge are in short supply.

Governmental decisions to keep permanent staff small have not helped Fuller. The Forest Service has begun contracting much of the actual trail construction. This means trail locators like Fuller must be more technical than if they were working with a crew of their own.

In laying out a trail, considerations must be given every rock outcropping, meadows that may be muddy, sudden downslopes, areas that may flood out after sudden rains. Every inch must be covered on foot by the locator. Details about each cutback, soil formation, and forest conditions must be explicit. It is hard work, but enjoyable. The pay is not the greatest, but, as Fuller will tell you, "I get by."

The Cleveland trails will eventually join with the Pacific Crest Trail, a 2,500 mile super-trail that will traverse the Pacific mountain ranges from the Mexican border to Canada. The super-trail will connect existing hiking trails, such as the John Muir Trail in the Sierra, and the Cascade Crest Trail in Washington.

Outdoor trails usually have been laid out for the strong of limb and heart. Naturalist John Olmstead thinks this is inappropriate. An official of Sausalito-based Sequoya Challenge, Olmstead has started a "Whole Access Trail" that can be enjoyed by disabled people as well as others.

Sequoya Challenge owns a parcel of land along the South Yuba River. The San Francisco Bay group used a ditch built by Excelsior Mines when the '49ers were sluicing gold from the Sierra foothills before California became a state. They have built a hard-packed trail that can be covered by those confined to wheelchairs, on crutches, or otherwise limited. All barriers have been removed, making it inviting to ablebodied and disabled alike.

Other private organizations similar to the nonprofit Sequoya Challenge and public agencies have joined in the enterprise. The Northern California Association of Four-Wheel Drive Clubs has helped in contruction of the trail. The state Department of Parks and Recreation and the Bureau of Land Management are involved. When the trail is completed sometime in 1982, BLM will assume responsibility for its management and up-keep.

Another who feels hiking is an appropriate activity is Lawrence Montgomery, who is walking across the whole breadth of the United States as this is written.

Montgomery's program, called "Hike-a-Nation," will lay out the path for a future hiking trail to open up the rural scene for city dwellers who have never experienced a hike in the country. The trail avoids cities. From Salt Lake City to Washington, D. C., it by-passes them all. This form of "low-energy recreation," Montgomery feels, is what people need to alert themselves to the beauty of the rural landscape and the danger of its demise should thoughtless people take charge.

Montgomery expects lots of company along the way. When he began his trek, ten thousand avid enthusiasts joined him crossing the Golden Gate Bridge on the first leg of his journey. He fully expects five thousand more to walk with him on other segments of his long walk.

A large educational movement is under way in the Golden State, in which young people learn by doing: the California

Conservation Corps (CCC). Grandfathers, uncles, and some parents will recall vividly and personally the original federal CCC, born in the Depression of the early 1930s, under the name Civilian Conservation Corps.

That CCC had several million members who were paid thirty dollars a month and given three meals a day, plus clothing and a cot in a tar-paper barracks. They, along with workers from the WPA (Works Progress Administration), performed wonders in clearing out woodlands, building bridges, and working on flood control. Members ranged in age from 17 to old-timers who were World War I veterans in their forties. The main purpose of the federal CCC was to give unemployed single men something to do.

The California Conservation Corps is as different as one can imagine. First it is *tough*! It is tough to get in, but it is tougher to stay in, and the responsibilities and expectations are high—very high. After a slow start, the CCC—California style—is making people sit up and take notice, particularly legislative doubters.

Gov. Jerry Brown on July 5, 1976, signed into law the legislation that created the CCC. Within its first three years, about 6,000 members took part in more than 3 million hours devoted to 1,440 public works and conservation projects. These works and projects included emergencies such as forest fires, floods, slides, snow removal, and search and rescue missions. They comprised reforestation and forest improvement (seed collection, propagation); fish and wildlife conservation (hatchery work, habitat enhancement); and soil and water conservation (erosion control, planting jojoba, guayule and grain amaranth).

Almost 7 percent of the workers' time was spent in fire hazard reduction, clearing brush, and maintaining fire trails along California's tinder-dry slopes. The CCC constructed and rehabilitated many public buildings and historical areas. And of course they built their own centers and renovated other centers rented from other public agencies.

A new program, needed but late in starting, included training for and conducting energy audits and installing solar panels for hot-water systems. By summer, 1980, the program was running full tilt and covered many solar applications.

To join the CCC one must be a resident of California, 18 to 23 years of age, willing to work hard to preserve the environment, and not be on probation or parole. The CCC encourages people with disabilities to join. Presently there are corps members who are deaf, blind, or have cerebral palsy. Women make up about one-third of the total enrollment of 1,824 members. The corps' ultimate goal is to have equal numbers of both sexes. There is a waiting list of one thousand names. Term of service is one year, although a corps member may leave at any time. Pay is $538 per month, from which $125 is paid back for room and board.

New enrollees—approximately three hundred each month—are sent to the Training Academy in the Sierra foothills, Calaveras County. Here they undergo nearly a month of intensive instruction on tool usage, woodsmanship, and worker safety. A rigorous training program is included and the recruits, many of whom have had no previous discipline, find their days long and hàrd. From an early 6 A.M. rising through calisthenics, breakfast, an 8 o'clock on-the-job start, to the close of the work day at 5 P.M., they are kept on the go constantly.

The success and impetus of the CCC can be laid at the doorstep of its hard-driving director, B. T. Collins. When asked what new members can expect out of the corps, Collins will answer in characteristic fashion, traces of New York City in his inflections, "I promise them nothing but hard work, low pay, and miserable conditions."

That last phrase, in fact, has been adopted as a slogan. The six words are emblazoned on the outside back cover of the latest CCC report to the California legislature. The front cover features a photo of a grime-covered young woman, weary after twenty-four hours of fighting forest fires in the searing heat of late summer. Below the cover portrait are three more words: "Character—Competence—Cooperation."

What rules cover corps members' daily lives? It is a simple table of commandments:

NO ALCOHOL

NO VIOLENCE

NO DRUGS

NO REFUSAL TO WORK

NO DESTRUCTION OF PROPERTY

Breaking any of these rules is grounds for termination.

CCC director Brian Thomas Collins has been called audacious, irreverent, outrageous, outspoken—but no one ever accused him of being a coward. He sports a hook in place of a right hand. He pumps along on an artificial right leg. Both of these amputations were caused by a grenade during his second tour of duty as an army captain in Viet Nam.

Collins is in his early forties. His curly hair is thinning at the temples, and his girth has broadened. But B. T. Collins is a bundle of energy who expects at least as much from the corps. "There is no reason why an eighteen- or nineteen-year-old can't work twelve to fourteen hours a day," he says.

He demands it and he gets it. Or the deficient corps member is "out." This has led to what some lawmakers see as a too-high rate of attrition. "That's caused by the nature of the program," Collins will say when asked. The attrition rate is especially high in the Calaveras Training Academy, where 20 to 30 percent drop out, or are dropped, from the academy.

This doesn't bother Collins, who feels the academy is a "shakedown," where screening is done for the first time. Col-

**California Conservation Corpsmembers clean streams of debris and logs.** (Photo courtesy CCC)

lins feels strictness is justified. Safety in forest work is important, as it is during rigorous fire-fighting efforts or working hip-deep in swirling floodwaters. And safety comes through discipline.

The "executive" building that serves Collins and his Sacramento staff was once an automobile agency at the corner of Sixteenth Street and Capitol Avenue, a brief walk from the State House. Window posters boast the corps' attitude:

IN THIS BUILDING WORK THE MEANEST, TOUGHEST, MOST DEDICATED CIVIL SERVANTS IN THE STATE OF CALIFORNIA!

Thus B. T. Collins spreads the fame of his CCC. Another sign taunts would-be corps members:

ONLY 38 PERCENT SURVIVED.
ARE YOU TOUGH ENOUGH?
ARE YOU GOOD ENOUGH?
TRY US, AND YOU'LL HATE US!

What makes the experience worthwhile to CCC members is found in their goals for 1980:

1. Accomplish 2 million hours of public service conservation work for the citizens of California.
2. Plant 2.5 million trees on public forestland in California.
3. Clear 60 miles of streams for salmon and steelhead spawning.
4. Propagate 150,000 native plants for use by public agencies for drought-tolerant landscaping and wildlife habitat enhancement.
5. Accomplish three major trail restoration projects in the national parks of California.

6. Ensure that 75 percent of available corps member work hours are spent on public service conservation work.
7. Reduce utility use by 25 percent at all CCC facilities. Reduce vehicle use by 15 percent. Reduce telephone use by 25 percent.
8. Train 50 corps members in the design, fabrication, and installation of solar panels.
9. Ensure that through the CCC's new literacy program all corps members, after their first year of service, are able to read and write at least at the sixth grade level.
10. Increase job placement for CCC graduates by informing the private sector—"corporate California"—that the CCC has mature and trained persons who are willing to work hard.

In striving for these goals, members find themselves reaching personal levels of leadership never hoped for. In qualifying for crew leadership, they receive 15 percent more pay. After their CCC service, seven crew leaders in 1979 entered the civil service system as conservationist technicians.

Other corps members may be given the unique opportunity to develop a particular, highly employable specialist skill.

These include:

- Cooking: Trained for planning and preparing meals for seventy-five to one hundred people.
- Energy conservation: Trained to conduct energy audits, perform remodeling for energy efficiency.
- Solar: Taught to design, fabricate and install solar heating systems.

A CC Corpsmember installing solar collectors on the roof of a park restroom to produce the hot water needed. (Photo courtesy CCC)

- Timber milling: Trained for management and operation of a small timber mill.
- Nursery: Trained in management and operation of a commercial nursery.
- Management: Trained in inventory control, farm and animal care, automotive maintenance, carpentry.
- Fire-fighting dispatch: Trained in air-weather, and deploying fire fighters where suppression warrants.

All CCC activities are considered simply as vehicles for developing the habit of active learning. The intangibles in-

**The CCC clears underbrush from forests and is on 24-hour alert for service in floods, forest fires, and other emergencies.** (Photo courtesy CCC)

clude a sensitivity to nature; the courage to face up to adversity, to control fear· actual knowledge, and the receptivity to knowledge.

The California legislature voted for five more years' funding in the spring of 1980. This pleases B. T. Collins. What pleases him more are his corps members. "They make me look good out there," he will confess in an unguarded moment. It is encouraging to know that California's wilderness trails, streams, forests, and deserts are in good hands. The CCC plan could be extended across the nation, and around the world. But help and dedication are required. Could this be your new career?

For You to Do Now:

Find a local volunteer program to beautify and protect the countryside, forest, or park land. Get close to nature for a time; climb a hill, go up a mountain, view the distance, think of yourself as part of nature. Join a hiking club.

Job Opportunities:

Fire fighter, flood controller, hydraulic engineer, timber miller, trail blazer, nursery worker, trail designer, stream restorer: AT jobs save the wilderness.

# CHAPTER 12
# AT IN MASS TRANSIT



THROUGHOUT HISTORY, modes of land transportation have varied; only in the past ten years has modern mass-transit management become a recognized profession. As such, it has attracted people from government, private industry, universities, and research consulting firms. All have a single quest: the perfect transit system. Only two aspects of future mass transit are certain: it will be multimodal, and it must be appropriate.

The transit systems grew as towns became cities. Travelers needed routes to follow from place to place. Merchants

169

required roads and vehicles to transport their goods. From antiquity, modes of transit varied from donkey to horse to carriage to tram. Before 500 B.C. stone-etched rutted roads were followed by travelers and freighters. It took over two thousand years for the wooden rail to be invented in England; the flanged wheel to ride the rails was invented in Germany.

The British wooden rails were set exactly 4 feet 8½ inches apart—a gauge still used in the New York City subway system. Iron wheels and track were substituted for wood in the eighteenth century. The first mode of public transportation in New York City was called the "omnibus," which dated back to France in 1819. The omnibus was a horse-drawn coach that held a dozen passengers.

In 1825 George Stephenson built the first steam railroad, in England. The first underground railway, or subway, was constructed in London, in 1855. New York's subway didn't come until 1912, although a man by the name of Alfred Ely Beach built a short underground pneumatic "tube" in 1870. The tube was closed up under orders from William Marcy ("Boss") Tweed, notorious Tammany Hall politician who had earlier thwarted the efforts of transit promoter Hugh B. Willson to build a subway. Tweed, it seems, was in the pocket of the omnibus interests, who at the time offered the sole method of public mass transit in New York City.

The omnibus and other horse-drawn carriages offered a bone-jarring ride over cobbled city streets. The coaches were poorly sprung, the wheels iron rimmed, the roadbeds generously dotted with holes and irregularities. The first American rail vehicle was also horse drawn. The Granite Railway began operation in Boston in 1826. Only six years later, the multicar trains of the New York and Harlem Railroad, all horse drawn, were on New York City streets. However, it wasn't until after 1850 that a streetcar boom began in earnest.

Brooklyn, Baltimore, Montreal, Philadelphia, New Orleans, Cambridge, Pittsburgh, Chicago, and Cincinnati had the first horse-powered street railroads within a matter of a few years. Soon every city in the United States boasted of its own streetcar system.

In August, 1873, the cable car made its debut on the hills of San Francisco. Soon this mode had its own mini-boom. Seattle, Chicago, Philadelphia, and New York all had highly successful cable-car runs. The cable over Brooklyn Bridge carried over 9 million passengers in its first nine months of operation. By 1900, most of the cable railways gave way to electric power. San Francisco has the only metropolitan cable-car system still in operation. It is maintained primarily as a tourist attraction.

One of the first heroes of electric transit was Frank Sprague. He devised the first trolley cars, in Richmond, Virginia. Sprague's first major installations were in Boston; from that time, about 1888, until the present, trolley cars have been extensively used to move people on urban and inter-urban lines.

Perhaps the most successful use of electric trolleys was found in the Los Angeles area between 1900 and the end of World War II. Here the giant Pacific Electric system transported billions of passengers over several million miles. In a twenty-year span, 1912–32, statisticians theorize Los Angeles trolleys carried 5.25 billion passengers over 600 million miles. But that was before the private passenger car had reached its zenith, and just before the gasoline-diesel bus made its indelible mark on urban transit.

Electric streetcars held on through the war years, until 1951, when they were taken out of production. By 1970, trolley cars could be found only in San Francisco, New Orleans, El Paso, Cleveland, Newark, Boston, Pittsburgh, Philadelphia, Toronto, and Cleveland. General Motors, Standard Oil of California, Firestone Rubber, and other suppliers were named by Bradford C. Snell, assistant counsel for the Senate anti-trust subcommittee, as conspirators to take over the electric transit systems in America and, in their place, install diesel bus fleets.

Nowhere was the result more evident, according to Snell in his 1974 report, than in southern California. Snell told of the change from Pacific Electric "Red Cars" paradise—green and gold, perfumed by orange blossoms and blessed with pure air—to a tawdry place spoiled by "noisy, foul-smelling" buses. He pointed out the 300 miles of freeways, the millions of private automobiles, the 13,000 tons of pollutants that daily fill the "septic-tank" air, killing palm trees and poisoning the people. He called the city of Los Angeles an "ecological wasteland."

No conspiracy was proved by the subcommittee. The general consensus among transit professionals is that systems as they exist today have little bearing on land use. However, many early streetcar and interurban rapid transit lines were designed to take people away from the center city. Lines often terminated at outlying amusement parks, new subdivisions, and suburban towns. Later transit lines—post 1960—were designed to bring suburbanites into city work places. Among these are the Bay Area Rapid Transit (BART), which runs from inland cities to San Francisco; part of the route is by underwater tube from Oakland. The Philadelphia Lindenwold line also brings commuters into the city.

Earlier transit lines added greatly to the sale of real estate and growth along the route. Later designs, however, apparently were installed more as a convenience to a small number of commuters than with real estate growth in mind. It can be assumed that new concepts will have little bearing on land use within the center city. Also, latter-day transit planners have merely furnished minimum transportation to tie population centers together. In other words, after suburban centers grew and residential neighborhoods demanded some service—usually minimal schedules for students, day workers, and casual shoppers—bus lines were drawn up seemingly as an afterthought.

Now the small world is in need of a Willson, a Beach, or a Sprague to come up with a new type of transit system for the twenty-first century. Without a doubt there are still many Boss Tweeds around to slow the wheels of appropriate progress, and many corporations to join selfishly with the omnibus combines who pay òff the Tweeds of this world. But something must be done to get the driver—particularly the American driver—out of his automobile.

The private automobile has made the American citizen dependent on gasoline he no longer can afford. And if the cost of gasoline is no barrier, he may be hooked on a fuel substance that no longer is available. Three generations of Americans have simply gotten out of the public-transportation habit, and into one almost impossible to break—the single-occupant automobile habit. There is no question that the individual enjoys the privacy of his own auto. That is why car-pooling has been only moderately successful. People want to get into their own vehicle, listen to their own radio or tape deck en route to business or shopping—or cruising—smoke or not at their own dictate, and share their space with whomever they choose.

Millions of residents in car-bound cities have never ridden on public transportation. They willingly suffer the scarcity of parking spaces, breathe auto emissions uncomplaining, wait in high-blood-pressure-inducing traffic jams as a matter of course. Their reward: independence on wheels! "The auto user's attachment to his machine has a fairly emotional base," says Jarold A. Kieffer, a Washington, D. C., transit authority. "It would have to be emotional, because it is plain that the average driver is aware of the mounting evidence that the continued use of cars under present city conditions is becoming almost counterproductive to him and his community."

Psychologists and transit planners call these emotions symptomatic of a malady called "transportation behavior":

> Transportation behavior represents a complex set of decisions made by individuals in which each person decides where and when to go, how often to go, and by which mode to go. The relationship between supply and the demand for transportation shows the aggregate total of the many individual decisions to travel.

Transportation problems exist where and when the transportation system can no longer provide for the smooth and efficient movement of people and goods. To eliminate transportation problems, public transportation planners must understand the imposing hold the private car has on the people they hope to wean away from their precious conveyances. "To attract automobile drivers to public transit without coercion," says J. Edward Anderson, professor of engineering at the University of Minnesota, "the transit trip must be faster than the auto trip for a significant number of trips made by urban residents."

Professor Anderson was not talking about more and bigger diesel buses. Neither are the entrepreneurs who are laying plans for future transit. Public transportation systems in most cities are currently operating near or beyond capacity during peak periods. Planners work diligently trying to form schedules that will take on more customers without raising costs. Capital outlays for more diesel buses stretch budgets beyond limits. Cries for federal assistance are heard in Washington. Some advocates plead for the return to street railways; "light rail" proponents form societies, and political activists gather at city council meetings to expound on their favorite mode of transit.

Alcohol distillers push strongly for their product to power all vehicles, private and public. Automotive engineers redesign internal combustion engines to function on 100 percent alcohol. Other entrepreneurs plan on marketing such locomotive means as the Hyde steam wheel and the stationary magnet.

One paper, prepared for the U. S. Department of Energy, titled "Investigation of the Feasibility of a Dual Mode Electric Transportation System," was published in 1977 by the Lawrence Berkeley Laboratory, University of California. "Dual mode" assumes the vehicles will be privately owned and operated. Using conventional styling, vehicles will be powered electrically. The energy is stored in battery packs under the hood in the space formerly occupied by the internal combustion engine.

When operated on standard residential streets, dual-mode vehicles run on battery power. On urban freeways and arterials, the power source is shifted from batteries to a power core buried under the road surface. Each traffic lane would have its own power core running the length of the power guideway. Electric energy would be transmitted through inductive power coupling, a method of magnetic transference. When the driver reaches the guideway, he flips a switch that drops a power pickup into place under the vehicle. This power pickup couples magnetically with electrical power from the center roadway source.

An air space of 2.5 centimeters separates the power pickup from the charged roadway, which gets its energy from conventional lines. The guideway, which has the function of a "third rail" in some systems and the trolley in others, is insulated and protected from traffic by a thick layer of non-conductive materials. This makes the powered roadway safe for incidental pedestrian traffic. As the vehicle runs on the electric roadway, the battery pack is automatically recharged. When changing lanes or leaving the roadway, the batteries take over.

To power these and other electric vehicles, batteries are being perfected that will replace the standard lead-acid type in use today. Leaders in this technological race are the lead-crystal and zinc-nickel-oxide types as well as lithium-sodium batteries. These have a longer life between charges (over 100 miles) and will last over 30,000 miles of driving. Recharging costs are minimal. Home chargers using photovoltaic cells will soon be available.

The greatest problem in urban transit is the congestion on city streets caused by privately operated vehicles. Dual-mode electrics do not help—in fact they could add to the problem if they became popular. However, another system of guided roadway transportation, called personal rapid transit (PRT), may provide an answer.

PRT systems consist of many small individual cars, publicly owned but privately operated on a "when required" basis. PRT vehicles have a load capacity of four adults. The rider travels either by himself or with companions of his own choosing.

Because PRT vehicles use guideways, no parking places are required on streets, and no public-access garages need be built. When not in actual use, PRT cars wait for riders at designated stations. During rush hours, each **PRT** vehicle is used on a number of round trips. **PRT** is a managed system, computer controlled, in contrast with present-day downtown traffic, which is completely disorganized, with drivers of varying competence vying for lanes and spaces.

A wide variety of transportation modes can be required by cities of different sizes and characteristics. A hilly city like Cincinnati, for instance, requires different modes than a flat city like Dallas. Cities with vast stretches of flat land surrounded by hills and mountains, such as found in Los Angeles, have separate needs. Certain options can suit all terrains and sizes.

One of these options is called "para-transit." A formal definition of para-transit was given in studies financed by the Urban Mass Transit Administration:

> Para-transit services are those forms of intraurban passenger transportation which are available to the public, are distinct from conventional transit (scheduled bus and rail), and can operate over the highway and street system.

This definition excludes the private automobile and systems such as PRT and dual mode, which require their own guideways. Para-transit includes taxis, jitneys, dial-a-ride, pool-vans and subscription buses. As a feeder service to line-haul transit (conventional transit of prescribed routes) para-transit can be invaluable.

Para-transit is suitable to areas with high-density home-to-work travel. Conversely, para-transit serves suburban and small towns well. Elderly persons and handicapped people as well as out-of-work people in search of employment can get excellent transportation from para-transit.

Other innovations such as "demand buses" fit the para-transit mode. Demand buses, usually van-type vehicles, seat eight or ten passengers. This nontracked bus, powered by electric batteries or hydrogen, is operated by a regular driver who keeps in constant touch with a computer-controlled bus terminal. As demands for transportation come into the control console, the driver receives the message simultaneously and goes to the spot of origin. On the way he may pick up other passengers who have called control. Each is taken to his own destination, which will be indicated when the call is made to control.

Demand buses are in effect a cross between a taxi and a conventional bus. The advantages over each are:

Direct door-to-door transportation from origin point to destination without transfers.
Economical rates for passengers.
Lower operating cost for transit company.
Reservations and adaptability are convenient for passengers.

Jitney service got its name from its cost when it first hit the American streets in 1914 and 1915. The fare was five cents—a "jitney" in street parlance. For a nickel a passenger could climb aboard and ride one block or ten, depending on the route and the desired destination. No schedules were kept or attempted.

Political pressures exercised by the street railways regulated jitneys out of business in most cities by the early 1920s. "Today only two fully legal jitney operations of significant size remain in the United States," writes Michael A. Kemp in the book *Para-transit,* "—Pacific Avenue in Atlantic City and Mission Street in San Francisco—although there are systems operating without formal authority in Chicago, Pittsburgh, Cleveland, Chattanooga, and almost certainly in other cities." A private jitney service in Anaheim, California, linking the baseball stadium, Disneyland, Knotts Berry Farm, and the commercial areas of Anaheim, was started in 1965.

Jitney vehicles are small, with a capacity of no more than twelve passengers. Current fares range between twenty and thirty cents. Passengers are picked up at specified stops, but may alight anywhere along the way. The service usually does not deviate from a given street or neighborhood, and there are no transfer privileges.

Planners are evaluating jitneys as a mode to shift automobile addicts away from their private wheels. Frequent, inexpensive, reliable (although nonscheduled) transportation along given city streets will offer casual shoppers and business commuters an alternative for the increasingly expensive and inappropriate private car and its parking problem.

Car pools, van pools, and subscription buses fit another mode of public transportation. Pool ridership is particularly successful in areas of high employment density, where groups of people from outlying areas travel to one central destination, such as a large factory, governmental complex, or business district. Shortage of parking space, extra costs such as bridge or highway tolls, and the heavy traffic concentration leading to traffic jams add to the desirability of pooling.

Some subscription buses are sponsored by employers; others are consumer-owned cooperatives. Nonprofit organizations, such as senior-citizen and community activist groups, operate small bus and van services. Most toll roads and bridges, as well as heavily traveled freeways, for instance around cities like Los Angeles and San Francisco, give all modes of para-transit vehicles right of way and free passage, thus offering two extra attractions: fast, unimpeded traffic flow and a cost incentive.

The sheer numbers of bus lines, regional transit districts, county and municipal carriers, and private transportation companies in the United States are staggering. The 1980 California transportation bus-carrier index alone lists 158 separate lines. The index does not include such interstate lines as Greyhound and Trailways; neither are charter lines nor individual charter carriers listed.

Nearly all bus carriers run on gasoline or diesel fuel. Researchers in hydrogen fuel (hydrides) are speaking confidently of breakthroughs in that technology. Methane gas, easily derived from raw municipal sewage and solid garbage waste, is aviand and city. Methanol and ethanol (alcohol) can be easily made from biomass. AT people feel this direction, together with retrofitting vehicles now in service where necessary to accept hydrides, methane or alcohol, will free the transit companies from the petroleum yoke.

The rapid strides taken by the solar-cell industry in producing silicon chips less expensively opens more avenues for investigation in the transit field. Researchers are already working on projects that include several of the para-transit modes listed above. One is a dial-a-ride car powered by solar cells with an improved battery backup. A customer would be picked up at the point of origin—for instance, at home. Others who live nearby and have the same approximate destination are picked up in the same vehicle. As in a share-the-ride taxi, each pays his separate fare or displays his monthly commuter's pass. All are destined for the same terminal point—bus transit stop, shopping center, business complex—and would disembark at the same place.

However, a more sophisticated mode may be added. Each car would have a magnetic coupling front and back by which it may form part of a train. Coupled, it would join other cars on an electric-powered guideway or, in some cases, an overhead monorail. The train would be destined for a more distant terminal. While the individual cars would be operated by a driver, the train would be computer controlled. When operating as a single car, the speed would adhere to surface street regulations.

When on the guideway or monorail, however, the train would accelerate to high speed. When reaching the end terminal, train cars would disengage from the magnetic hookup. New drivers would chauffeur passengers to individual destinations. This would be true door-to-door transportation with high-speed applications.

During the guideway or monorail trip, the car's individual batteries would be recharged, if necessary, automatically. Top surfaces of the car—roof, battery hood, trunk areas —would be plated with solar-cell collectors. Excess power would be fed to the guideway en route. Such door-to-door convenience at moderate prices could be an excellent selling point in the attempt to help the American driver break his private-vehicle addiction.

FOR YOU TO DO NOW:

Attend public meetings of your local transit authority. Take an extended ride on your local bus or streetcar system. Note the areas not serviced by public transit. As a class project, or with a group of friends, design an appropriate transportation system for your town or city.

JOB OPPORTUNITIES:

Whatever the mode of transportation, many jobs will open up within the public transit sector: mechanics and operators; supervisors, clerks, and cashiers; designers, engineers, and all the secondary support necessary to keep a large company in operation.

# CHAPTER 13

# AT IN DROUGHT AND FAMINE

*IF YOU GIVE A MAN A FISH,
YOU FEED HIM FOR A DAY.
IF YOU TEACH HIM TO FISH,
YOU FEED HIM FOR
A LIFETIME.*

—ANCIENT PROVERB—
THE LIKLIK BUK
PAPUA NEW GUINEA, 1977

DROUGHT and famine. History books and current journals hold many tales of horror, terror, and misery brought on by these phenomena. Throughout the climb of civilization, scientists have attempted to uncover the causes and lessen the effects of drought and famine. With its collective expertise, Western science tries to surmount the ravages of wind and excessive sun; of flood and erosion; of pestilence and war.

Often we muddle through. Sometimes we are successful. Sometimes we produce chaos. Advanced technologies, those that rely heavily on fossil fuels, nuclear reactors, and sophisticated computer systems, are stopped dead when confronted by the awesome power of nature. Hurricane winds, rumbling earthquakes, erupting volcanoes: these reduce man and his technology to an elementary state, commensurate with his ability to cope. Then, once a crisis has been passed, inappropriate technologies again push into the forefront.

Some of the Western nations' problems are of our own making. They "sneaked up" when we were not looking. The Western world's dependency on Middle Eastern oil, for instance, to keep an economy alive, resulted in an inflation-depression that few were prepared for.

More subtle still have been the results of modern technology in relation to the ecosystem. Scientists have only recently become aware of the effects of insecticides, herbicides, and other chemical compounds used in a variety of ways. For the past ten years, almost too late, studies have revealed their shortcomings, and steps are being taken to correct their misuse. Researchers have been seeking methods to replace all-purpose technologies, hoping for foolproof biological means of controlling blight and infestations that interrupt the food supply worldwide.

Often these global questions and their technological answers are not understood by Western nations. Climate control—or weather modification, as it is often called—fits that category well. There are methods of seeding clouds over regions where rainfall is desperately needed to save crops. Farmers petition atmospheric scientists for their services. Sometimes results are disastrous. On June 9, 1972, the South Dakota School of Mines and Technology seeded the clouds in the vicinity of Rapid City, South Dakota. The operation, under contract with the Department of the Interior, was called Project Skywater.

Within a few hours an intense downpour brought on a flash flood that inundated thousands of acres, causing untold misery and millions of dollars in damage to fields, livestock, and buildings. The debates are still going on as to whether the flood was caused by natural means or by weather modification.

On July 29, 1980, downpours sent water surging 10 feet deep through Smryna, Delaware. Officials seeking to help farmers stricken by a long drought had seeded the clouds the night before. But state officials, including Agriculture Secretary Alden Hopkins, said the downpour had nothing to do with cloud seeding. Delaware farmers are seeking redress.

The courts decide such matters in the United States. But what if the seeding had occurred near an unfriendly international border? What courts could decide payment of damages? Could a war start over cloud seeding? Could cloud seeding be used as a war tool? Is cloud seeding an appropriate technology to fight drought? It is such difficult international questions that Western nations seem unable to comprehend.

Some Western scientists say the world's hunger problems would be lessened through population control; by raising the gross national product (GNP) of backward countries; by bringing up the literacy rate; by pushing food production.

However, recent world history shows these methods do not necessarily work. First, cultures in the world's poorest countries do not accept easily the well-intended efforts of Western scientists to cut down birthrates. Secondly, social changes, when they do come to developing countries, often do the unexpected opposite.

Rich landholders, with new methods that include high-yield seed strains, better irrigation methods, insecticides and adequate fertilizers, have realized substantially increasing yields and income—all thanks to Western technology. The small farmer, who often relies on the large landholder for subsistence, remains small, not enjoying the success of his larger, now prosperous neighbor.

Two international organizations deeply concerned with the hungry people of this small world are the World Health Organization (WHO) and the International Bank for Reconstruction and Development, known as the World Bank, or the bank. Both organizations offer excellent career possibilities for AT people interested in the essential human needs of all groups in society.

The World Bank was founded at the Economic Conference held at Bretton Woods, New Hampshire, in July, 1944. Its original emphasis was on lending funds for reconstruction; in later years, the bank devoted its efforts toward economic development.

WHO, on the other hand, was established to help all people attain the highest possible level of health. WHO began functioning officially on September 1, 1948, three years after it was proposed at the original San Francisco Conference on International Organization, at which the United Nations was founded. WHO will help governments, on request, to strengthen health services, and furnish technical assistance. This may include promoting nutrition, improving sanitation, or correcting working conditions and other aspects of environmental hygiene. WHO has undertaken control of epidemics and attempted to eradicate diseases such as malaria, tuberculosis, syphilis, influenza, cholera, yaws, rabies, and has even helped combat alcoholism and mental illness.

At the beginning, the World Bank worked the economic side of the street. It had funded only tangible projects; in later years it made loans for more abstract programs. These programs include vocational and technical education and population control, as well as lending funds for urban water supply and sewerage improvements, all aimed at improving the quality of life rather than increasing the economic output in a developing country.

Although WHO and the World Bank can point to remarkable progress in the alleviation of disease, famine, and suffering throughout the world, their biggest problems have yet to be solved. These difficulties have their roots in the proportion of children in the population of developing countries. According to a 1980 World Bank report, more than 250 million children and 600 million adults still lack basic education. The number of children is increasing so rapidly that resources cannot meet the demand for education.

Women have not been offered the same educational opportunities in many countries; this contributes to the problem. Inefficiencies in administering education programs have also kept down the quality of education and depressed enrollment levels.

The World Bank and WHO welcome expertise in many areas. Engineers are in demand: civil, mechanical, electrical, sanitary, hydraulic—any type of engineering degree and experience can expect acceptance in both organizations. Agronomists, livestock managers, marketing experts, and economists are needed in the worldwide agricultural industry.

Almost all World Bank and WHO field employees are engaged in some sort of advisory capacity and work in close cooperation with the leaders in the developing country where the mission, project, or program is centered. Americans work on teams with citizens of other member nations, assisting governments as requested. Their duties often take them far from home, to places of uncertain political balance where cultures differ dramatically from those in the United States.

Patience seems to be the strongest virtue when working in underdeveloped countries. Successes are slow in coming.

Some countries attempt to emerge into the world of economic parity through independent action. In Tanzania, a country roughly the size of Texas, 14.5 million people have been moved into communal villages. None of the villages is more than 5 miles from water. Only one thousand villages have been supplied with on-site water resources. This means in seven thousand villages the people have to carry the water themselves, in any container they can get, sometimes as far as 5 miles.

Political problems with neighboring Kenya have lessened Tanzania's chances of full-scale international help. More than 90 percent of their working population depends on agriculture, and water, to bring in 80 percent of its export earnings. Droughts from 1973 to 1975 were disastrous, forcing the government to import over half a million tons of grain. In the winter of 1979, the drought continued, and Tanzania's trade deficit grew to over $600 million.

Meanwhile, in the state of Uttar Pradesh, one of India's most populous, villagers grub for roots and berries to keep from starving. Although the 1980 famine is not as bad as that in Cambodia, or in Africa's Sahel region ten years ago, there is not enough food being distributed to the needy. Yet there is a reserve of 20 million tons of grain in central government warehouses. So India's worst drought of the century has forced landless farm workers into near starvation. Richer farmers of the district get water for their lands, while the rest of the fields dry up and blow away in the hot winds.

Perhaps the most pressing problem of the Third World and of much of the Western world, is the rehabilitation of arid lands, according to permaculturist Bill Mollison of Tasmania, the island state off Australia. Mollison hopes for the day when the landless farmers will be able to produce their own food on plots rehabilitated from eroded, soilless places where trees have been cut down and the ground has been allowed to dry. This is a gigantic task, one that will require the utmost in cooperation from all governments and leaders.

"Once the trees have been totally removed, the goat and camel flocks have killed all regrowth, and the soil blown away, reforestation is a problem," Bill Mollison says. However, he declares, trees act as natural climate controllers, causing clouds to form and natural rainfall to be increased.

As large a job as it seems, land rehabilitation is possible, and AT people all over the world are succeeding in this effort. Some advisers are from the World Bank, some from WHO, and some work for independent organizations, most of them nonprofit. Using ancient Chinese methods, and those of certain native North American tribes who farm with virtually no rainfall, agriculturists have learned how to subdue drifting sand dunes, drill holes for orchards on stony hillsides, make sheet-plastic "wells" to hold water, or to condense enough water from the dry night air to keep a tree alive or water a plant or two.

Plants that are properly arranged can keep themselves strong, their nutrients recycled among them. Crops are mulched from leaves and branches of trees, which hold the leached nutrients in an underground root web. Branches and leaves fed to livestock are returned to field crops as manure; legumes and pulses form ground cover for root and grain crops. Trees act as barriers for invading weeds.

Building up the deprived soil from leaf and dung mulches is a long process. But it is possible. When finally successful, people become self-sufficient, and a healthy, stable community emerges.

Drought can create hardships even in the more sophisticated urban areas in the Western world. People who have taken water supply for granted all their lives are dumbfounded when told there may not be enough on tap for lengthy showers, hosing down sidewalks, and washing cars.

California, long noted for vast water reserves, private swimming pools, lush gardens and green lawns was rudely awakened in 1977 when rainfall fell below normal levels for the second consecutive year. Reservoir lakes filled to overflowing by snow runoff in normal years were so low that boats were removed to keep them from becoming stuck in the mud of drying lake bottoms. Fish died in batches; wildfowl changed migratory habits.

Soon the Department of Water Resources called for a concerted effort by all citizens to conserve water. They regulated the amount of water to flush toilets. They used low-flow shower heads, and saved their dirty bath and dish water (called "gray water") for their plants and vegetables. In some cases, lawns were permitted to dry up entirely; in others, certain days were allotted for watering grass and shrubbery. Automobiles could not be washed on the street; the soapy runoff had to occur on lawn areas so as not to be wasted. Some individuals accepted the drought as a good excuse not to wash their cars at all.

A modern-day aqueduct was devised to get water from Contra Costa County to Marin County. The San Francisco Bay lies between the two counties. A large pipe was devised to carry fresh water over the San Raphael-Richmond bridge. Marinites were assured of enough water to survive until the rains came.

The most important product of California's drought years was an awareness of the need to conserve water, in other states as well as California. To help spread this awareness the state Office of Appropriate Technology, with the help of Water Resources and the Forestry Department, created a "drought garden" on a vacant corner lot not far from the state Capitol.

The Drought Garden, later to be renamed the Urban Water Conservation Garden, was developed as a demonstration for people who wanted to know about designing, building, and maintaining a landscape that conserves water and other resources. In 1980, the garden management was turned over to a local mental health group, the Community Interaction Program, which also has a solid-waste recycling program close by.

The garden has turned out to be an excellent source for ideas about home and park landscaping that provides food, recreation, and a pleasant variety of settings—as well as open space for a downtown neighborhood. The lot is approximately 90 by 135 feet and runs north and south. The northern half contains a gazebo, patio, and barbecue designed as a home landscape. The southern half of the lot is designed to show how a typical vacant corner can be transformed into a functional, attractive park using drought-tolerant native and exotic plants.

Public tours are held periodically, during which visitors are taught the benefits of careful planning for various soils and climates. They hear about mulching, irrigation systems, erosion prevention; they learn how permeable paths such as decomposed granite help keep water in the garden, not in the gutter. Gardeners learn about building compost boxes and using the product for improving the soil's quality. A small demonstration section is reserved for vegetables. Here neighbors may plant some tomatoes, or beets, herbs and flowers. A small fruit orchard—pear, peach, plum, apricot, orange, olive, almond, pomegranate, loquat—is placed in a center section. Neighbors get the fruit crop.

A selection of flowers, colorful annuals that are hardy and grow well in their seasons, keeps the Drought Garden bright with bloom all year. Certain areas not used for active recreation have been planted with drought-resistant ground cover instead of concrete or grass. In an area adjacent to a three-story apartment building, shrubs have been planted for screening, color, form, and texture. A fast-growing Italian buckthorn forms an informal hedge and screen. A sunlit rock garden is a focal point. It holds river rock, with colorful lichen, accented by the blue-green foliage of yucca and blue fescue. Aromatic thyme, creeping Peruvian verbena, and succulents are spread among the rocks and mounds.

Several irrigation methods are being tested and used in different areas of the Drought Garden—soaker hose, a drip system with small emitter tubes, small-ditch irrigation. None are overused, and no water is ever wasted. Wide beds allow maximum use of the growing area, and narrow, defined pathways prevent soil compaction.

It is a quiet, restful island in a sea of busy city life. People from nearby office buildings will stroll in for a short lunch break. A religious advocate may sit yoga-style for an hour of meditation on the small lawn area. Elderly folks from neighboring housing units use the garden as a meeting place, or as a rest stop on their marketing tours. The greatest benefit of the Urban Water Conservation Garden is its presence, small though it is. People talk about it after visits; others read about it. Many emulate it. Everyone who loves growing things despite drought problems is impressed by what can be grown. The garden is a highly appropriate activity, one whose philosophy will spread with time.

Agriculturists have worked diligently in their search for seed strains that will have greater yield. Almost unheralded, however, are the fish biologists who are using new technologies to

**Seniors work and stroll through the Urban Garden, which was once a trash-filled corner lot.**

raise seafood. Fish, high in protein and varied in flavor, have been a human diet mainstay for many generations along the world's seaboards and wherever freshwater lakes abound. Toxic poisons, oil spills, and other forms of pollution have decimated fish production around the globe. Scientists are experimenting with controlled methods of raising seafood in "ranches" near oceans or far inland. The biologists who built Solar AquaSystems have been followed by others trying similar methods.

Piscatorial pioneer Dr. George Allen, in the first experiment of its kind, has used treated sewage to raise thousands of coho salmon at Humboldt State University, along the northern California coast. About 60 million pounds of salmon have been produced a year in public hatcheries in Oregon, Washington, and Alaska, where they have been caught in public waters by commercial fishermen. The United States currently imports more than half of the fish consumed in the country, according to the National Academy of Science. But there has been no increase in the catch since 1970. Dr. Allen hopes to tie his experimental ranch into the sewage system in Arcata, a nearby coastal city of 10,000, and later into other neighboring communities. His plans, when successful, would utilize sewage from all coastal cities, raising the salmon catch immeasurably.

Sixty miles south of the Arizona border in Puerto Penasco, Mexico, researchers from the University of Arizona and the University of Sonora have joined forces to build a pilot shrimp-growing operation—not on the Gulf of California, as one would expect, but inland, away from the water. Eventually a commercial facility will be capable of producing 80,000 to 100,000 pounds of shrimp per acre, per year. A domed environment, similar to Solar AquaSystems installations, will lead to a more efficient harvest and more uniformly sized shrimp. Shrimp boats working out of Puerto Penasco can capture only a fraction of the amount planned at the seafood farm. Shrimp harvested will be fresher, frozen immediately after being removed from the water.

More seafood wonders are predicted by scientists from the University of California at their Bodega Bay installation, the Marine Laboratory. One of their pet projects is lobster farming. Some people question the propriety of spending time and money on developing a luxury food item like lobsters. "Yes, this is a romantic, luxury item," researchers admit. "But the investment money is going to be spent on the hardware and on the engineering, and the system can then be used throughout the world on any species whatever. It is a great contribution to mankind."

The researchers recognize that we are protein poor in only certain countries. But they also realize that the tremendous costs of developing aquaculture must come from the wealthy companies and speculators in economically strong countries. Ultimately lobster research and farming will pay a good share of fish-farm development in other areas.

The Bodega Marine Laboratory is hidden behind huge sand dunes on Bodega Head, a large headland that juts out into the Pacific Ocean about 60 miles north of San Francisco. Reached by an unprepossessing road, the lab straddles the infamous San Andreas Fault, the earthquake nemesis of California. The fault, in fact, lies directly under the narrow blacktopped road that leads from Bodega Bay through brush-covered dunes to the ocean-front laboratory.

Once at the lab, the view is breathtaking. A narrow strip of grassy park land separates the main building from the crashing surf which beats against the rocks only feet below. The office of Dr. Douglas E. Conklin, associate director of the aquaculture program, looks out on such a panorama of beauty that one wonders how he can concentrate on his project.

Conklin can, and does, you realize after a tour of the lobster lab. Here tier after tier of lobsters from the tiniest specimens to large, ready-to-eat monsters, are available for study. Conklin's specialty is "invertebrate nutrition." The National Sea Grant College Program sponsors research at the marine lab. This program can be compared to the Land Grant College Program, established in 1865, which has been instrumental in helping the United States become the world's leading agricultural nation.

Daily feeding of the laboratory's lobsters consists of a recently developed purified diet containing 8 percent lecithin, and comes in a dry, extruded mass-produced pellet in which optimum nutrient levels can be supplied. Because lobsters are cannibalistic from the day of hatching, each must have its own compartment. In order to maintain high growth rates, animals—including lobsters—must be allowed free movement. As soon as they outgrow one compartment, they must be shifted to the next size. It is a constant activity.

Two groups have been building pilot plants in order to test the economic feasibility of commercial lobster aquaculture: Sanders Associates, Inc., of Nashua, New Hampshire, and the Southern California Edison Company of Rosemead, California. Computer figures show that if a facility could produce 1 million pounds per year, consisting of 80,000 1-pound lobsters per month, requiring a capital investment of $3 million, it may be successful. We asked Dr. Conklin if these ambitious and very expensive enterprises did not tempt him away from his laboratory and research into the realm of big business. "They can't afford to duplicate my view," he smiled, pointing to his office windows. "I think I'll stay here."

These seemingly far-out and expensive research projects

may appear extraneous in the desperate battle against famine and drought in this small world. Yet it is through research that the answers to these serious questions must be found.

A more esoteric solution may have been found at Marsh Farms, a San Diego breeding "factory" for Coturnix quail. Fowl—notably chickens—are recognized internationally as an excellent protein source for hungry people in emerging countries. Coturnix quail, domesticated in Egypt six thousand years ago, could take the lead from the accepted barnyard bird within the next few years, if Al Marsh has his way.

Al Marsh started his multimillion-dollar enterprise with a couple of quail behind his sofa in an apartment. Now he

**Dr. Douglas E. Conklin, associate director of the Bodega Marine Lab, University of California, checks moulting lobster. Naturally cannibalistic, lobsters must have separate compartments and are moved to larger ones as they grow.**

breeds them by the thousands—together with pheasants and turkeys—on his southern California acres. These charming little birds have only one fault: they are too cute to eat, once you have raised them from their embryonic stage. But if you can forget sentiment, quail and their eggs have much in their favor as a human nutrient.

Foremost is their ability to reproduce. Six weeks after hatching, the females begin laying eggs, tiny things about one-quarter the size of hens' eggs. They can produce an egg a day with uncanny reliability. Two dozen fertilized eggs will yield one thousand quail within a year, plus a quarter of a million eggs.

While Marsh Farms furnishes a recommended diet for their fowl, the quail are not fussy. "They will eat any grain or seed," Stuart Berman, a Marsh Farms quail handler, told us. "And they will eat any bug in sight." Berman cautions about feeding table scraps to the plump little birds, but said they will eat raw vegetable scraps readily, and they can keep a garden area weed free.

Quail are very tame. If they get daily care, they will not fly away; they show no fear of humans. Their meat is tastier than chicken, and more tender than wild quail.

Marsh sells most of his egg production to the Asian markets where, when pickled, they are considered a delicacy. Quail eggs are popular in the international set as an hors d'oeuvre, and can be found in Oriental bars from Tokyo to Hong Kong.

However, it is toward the hungry nations that Marsh is directing his efforts. He furnishes breeding quail, a cage large enough to hold three, a small incubator, and directions for feeding and care; fertilized eggs are three dollars a dozen; week old chicks are two dollars each. His best customer so far has been Saudi Arabia, which has recently purchased one hundred incubating units. Every sixteen days twenty thousand new quail will hatch in Saudi Arabia. "We hope to send our message around the world," Berman told us. "Quail can be a very important food resource."

This, too, can be called an appropriate technology.


FOR YOU TO DO NOW:

Think of ways you and your family can save water. Find out where your water supply originates. Research local annual rainfall tables. Imagine you must survive with a small fraction of the amount. If possible, plant a drought garden.


JOB OPPORTUNITIES:

Fowl breeder, invertebrate nutritionist, oceanographer, weather modifier control; every category of professional and nonprofessional career can be found in WHO and the World Bank projects.

# CHAPTER 14

*THERE ARE NO UTOPIAS IN THE OFFING . . . BUT MAN COULD CREATE A SANER, HAPPIER, LESS ALIENATED AND MORE HUMANE WORLD.*

BILL MOLLISON
PERMACULTURE TWO, 1979

# AT THROUGHOUT THE WORLD

YOUR CAREER search may take you all around this small world. You will learn of places where AT is practiced as a way of life, or is in the experimental stages.

You may be surprised to find that Greece is building the world's largest solar energy plant, producing 20 megawatts of electric power, in cooperation with the West German Ministry of Scientific Research and Technology.

Japan, realizing a continuing dream of researchers for almost 200 years, in 1978 set up an experimental station near

Honshu Island to produce 125 kilowatts from wave power. A floating chamber causes air to be pushed through nozzles in the top of the chamber, turning air turbines that drive electric generators.

British designers have come up with another wave-generator, called "contouring rafts." These three-section rafts are hinged together. The flexing of the hinges through wave action forces pistons to pump water that turns turbines. A cluster of 300 or more rafts could rival a large conventional power station's output.

Hawaii too has extracted energy from the sea. A floating power plant generates one million watts of electric power. In the system a working fluid vaporizes at low temperature when surrounded by frigid waters piped up from ocean depths. The pressurized vapor drives a power-generating turbine. Efficiency tests will be completed by 1982.

Another inventor wants to use the sea in an entirely novel way. Joseph A. Connell, of Los Angeles, plans to move icebergs from the antarctic to the African deserts. Once there, the ice would be melted for irrigation.

Connell says 430 cubic miles of icebergs break loose from the polar cap each year. These hold more pure, uncontaminated fresh water than all the earth's rivers. The idea is to select a large berg—antarctic bergs are flat on top, not peaked as their northern cousins are—put aboard a crew of 40 or 50, plus equipment, and pump Freon into heat exchangers submerged beneath the ocean surface. Temperature changes between the berg and the sea would expand the gas, which in turn would spin propellers, driving the iceberg far enough to hit the Humboldt current. The warmer Humboldt, which runs from the tip of South America to the equator, would increase the speed to four knots. When the "craft" reached its destination it would be harbored in a plastic cocoon, which would keep the fresher, lighter melting water from escaping to the sea.

Cost of the initial trip would be $65 million; subsequent voyages a mere $15 million. Consumer costs would be less than seven cents per thousand gallons, which compares favorably with ten cents per thousand gallons of irrigation water.

Another method of using iceberg water was studied by the Saudi Arabians, who thought they might tow the huge ice-cubes. However, the cost of 8 to 10 tugs using about 100 million gallons of fuel caused the Saudis to reconsider.

There is some evidence that Saudi Arabia would like to see solar cities bloom in its open desert. At least that is the vision of Dr. George Abi-Rached, a mechanical engineer and contractor. Abi-Rached says he would prefer to have the oil remaining under Arabian sand be utilized by the petrochemical industry, rather than having it burned for energy that could just as well be obtained from the sun. The engineer declares that the oil supply could run out in 20 years, while the sun will always be heating Arabia.

Solar pond technology, another appropriate technology, came true in Israel in 1980. The tiny desert community of Ein Bokek near the southern shore of the Dead Sea, received its first 150 kilowatts of power from a shallow (8 feet deep) salt-laden pond just 70,000 square feet in area. That is the equivalent land measurement of the space inside a quarter-mile oval running track.

Solar pond electrical generators consist of salt water, a heat-exchanging system, and a turbogenerator. The salt in the water will sink to the bottom. When heated by the sun, it will not rise above the fresher top water, and soon traps enough heat energy to raise the temperature to 176° Fahrenheit. The hot water is funneled into the tubes of the heat-exchanger, which is surrounded by a low-boiling-point liquid. The heat vaporizes the liquid within its tubes; the pressure turns the turbine. When the process is over, the cooled liquid returns to the heat-exchanger to be vaporized again and again. Nothing is lost in the process.

Israeli scientists plan for larger ponds, estimated construction cost approximately $2,000 per kwh, about the cost of a hydroelectric plant.

Delft University of the Netherlands has a multi-disciplinary center for appropriate technology whose project-initiative activities include a solar ice-production unit, a sugar manufacturing furnace, a hydrolic ram, protein production from agricultural waste, water purification, and a substitute for cement.

According to Delft literature, their approach offers a diverse integration, representing technological, social, cultural and economic aspects. "Without doing this, one can hardly speak of a really *appropriate* technology approach," they say.

Agreeing with this multi-disciplinary approach but at a grass-roots level is Volunteers in Technical Assistance (VITA), a private, non-profit organization which supports people working on technical problems in developing areas.

"VITA offers information and assistance aimed at extending the ability of institutions and individuals to select and implement technologies appropriate to their particular situations." So states their quarterly magazine, VITA *News*.

VITA volunteers make their presence known around the world, working on technology transfer—the movement of technical information, equipment, and so forth, from one place to another—and technology diffusion—the adaptation and adoption of these procedures.

VITA's commitment is to act as a transfer agent or a diffusion partner wherever it is asked for assistance. This takes them to Central America to build a cannery; to South America to design a cable bridge; to Africa to erect a windmill; to India to set up solar cookers.

A group in England calls themselves the Network for Alternative Technology and Technology Assessment (NATTA). It was set up in 1976 to provide a forum for discussion and communication between individuals and groups active in the alternative energy field. NATTA fears the world might close its options by putting all its eggs in the nuclear basket. It promotes dialogue on such alternatives as small wind power units (3 mw maximum), wave power and solar collectors.

Of all the developing countries throughout the world, the new nation of Papua New Guinea (PNG) must be recognized as adapting itself to AT philosophy.

PNG is a composite made up of 600 islands, organized administratively into 20 provinces. The scattered populace is multifarious: 750 different languages are spoken, one-fourth of the languages spoken in the world. Certain ethnic groups have no more than several dozen members. Three languages have acquired official status: Motu, the commercial language; Neo-Melanesian (Pidgin); and English, the technical language.

In most areas neither the wheel nor metal technologies are used, and irrigation is not practiced.

Only 10 percent of Papua New Guineans live in the market economy sector; this includes technicians, administrators, and those working in commerce and on plantations. The balance of the people live in self-sufficient villages.

PNG acquired its independence on September 16, 1975,

after a five-year period of administrative autonomy under Australian jurisdiction.

As PNG advanced into its own political sphere, it was deemed necessary to preserve not only the land, but the cultures of this technologically rudimentary people. With the blessings of the Office of Village Development, the Department of the Environment, and the Central Planning Office from the governmental sector, and with the help of the University of Papua New Guinea, the South Pacific Appropriate Technology Foundation (SPATF) was started in 1976.

PNG appropriate technologies were described as:

1.  More reliant on local material
2.  Less capital intensive
3.  More adaptable to local skills
4.  Less disruptive of traditional customs
5.  Less destructive of the environment
6.  More conducive to local initiative and local control
7.  *Much* less capital intensive

As in all South Pacific countries today, PNG has its "modern sector" in the cities. It is dependent on the expertise and goods provided by foreigners either as experts or suppliers. High-level technologies are implanted by entrepreneurs who knock on the doors of the politicians attracted by the lure of a part share, or by promise of a greater tax base.

The evils of this traditional colonial development pattern are evident wherever villagers leave home for the spurious cash inducements offered by high level technology enterprises. City slums become jammed with village people with inadequate skills, worthless in high-tech circles. It is a scene familiar to any world-traveler.

To save its citizens a similar fate, with a push in the

proper direction by SPATF, the PNG government stressed at the South Pacific Conference on Economic Development (October 1976) that: "the technology is often very wrong. International market forces and community prices and lending agencies often force adoption of inappropriate technologies by developing countries." The PNG government then advocated "ecodevelopment" as the only viable alternative for itself, as well as all the nations of the South Pacific. SPATF brought the following point forward in their original proposal:

> It is strongly argued that there is a need for the transfer of technology to villagers to enable them to increase their production and to improve their way of life. The transfer of appropriate skills and small scale machinery will enable the village people to rely more on themselves and at the same time enable them to participate in the modern economy from a position of strength. All kinds of activities employing these new skills will once again make the village a meaningful place to live. At the moment, in many cases, it is merely a place to leave once the opportunity comes.

While the Papua New Guineans have been planning for their own futures and the futures of the rest of the South Pacific nations, a tiny group over 2000 miles directly south in Tasmania, an island state off the southern coast of Australia, has been quietly working on the future of the world.

They call themselves "Tagari."

Tagari is a non-profit foundation of about 30 parents, single people and children devoted to the evolution of the meta-industrial village, patterned after William Thompson's model in *Darkness and Scattered Light.*

Tagari's concept is called "Permaculture."

Their spokesman, one of their founders and author of *Permaculture II*, is Bill Mollison. He is a quiet, strong man of modest size but giant commitment to the philosophy of Permaculture, which is, in brief, a philosophy of working with, rather than against, nature.

Permaculture is a way of life, a way of growing things, a way of raising animals, a way of preserving the land, a way of making the land do the work, rather than depending on "protracted and thoughtless labor," according to Mollison.

The main thrust in Permaculture is toward perennial crops, away from annual crops; it leans toward small farms, away from large, energy inefficient, corporate tracts.

On the same amount of acreage, Mollison shows that more crops—including wood, nuts, fruit, grains and vegetables—can be harvested through Permaculture methods than by the accepted "big farm" monoculture method.

Following the teaching of the ancients, from the aborigines to Virgil, Tagari has learned the complex relationship between animal and vegetable species, water and land. They lean heavily on the works of other gardeners: Ruth Stout and M. Fukuoka each have written extensively on similar theories.

1. *No cultivation*—do not turn the soil over.
2. *No chemical fertilizer or prepared compost*—let the plants and animals that make the soil go to work on the soil.
3. *No weeding by tillage or herbicide*—use the weeds; control them by natural means, or occasional cutting.
4. *No dependence on chemicals*—insects and disease, weeds and pests, have their own controls; let these operate, and assist them.

Mollison and his friends prepare a garden by "sheet mulching," which begins with laying dolomite with chicken manure or blood and bone meal over untilled ground. The quality of the ground does not matter. They cover it with successive layers of overlapped cardboard or newspapers or both, straw, and raked leaves. After watering down well, seeds are burrowed into the resulting mulch. Transplanted seedlings are placed through slits in the cardboard or newspaper.

"O. K.," Mollison says. "Instant garden. Time to retire."

If the materials are at hand, he can set out a garden, 30 feet square, in less than half an hour. And it works!

By the end of the first summer after sheet mulching, the soil will be revolutionized; it will contain hundreds of worms and beneficial soil bacteria. A little top mulch added will keep levels up—usually a mix of chips, bark, pine needles, hay—and the "waste" from all vegetables is "tucked under" the mulch. It all becomes part of the cycle. Worms are so active that the leaves and peelings disappear overnight.

We have described this "effortless" method of gardening because it is the heart of Permaculture.

With intentional communities of limited size, and many small gardens set out in many small areas of the world, Mollison believes the world would soon be self-sustaining, with no need for heavy equipment and petroleum.

Wood products would become as plentiful as vegetables. Small ponds would give a bounty of fresh fish and crustaceans. Fibers for clothing would be reaped in abundance. And natural nutrients would be preserved, not lost through poor monoculture management.

Permaculture would not be reserved for special places in the world where things grow easily.

Mollison's designs include arid lands, as well as tropical

and coastal regions, as these are of greater extent in Australia, and the Third World. His plans work on rocky terrain, on hillsides, in the humid tropics and at the seaside.

We hazarded another question about this seemingly utopian way of life—although Mollison does not offer utopia —and wondered about employment in an economy that relied on many small producers.

"You would be guaranteed no unemployment," Bill Mollison assured us. "There would be so much to do, so many ways to achieve salable, valuable products, that a shortage of help would be indicated, not the reverse."

There would be no waste, according to Mollison, including human beings.

In retrospect, it is easy to agree with the Permaculture theory. To begin with, such teachers and designers as Mollison would be in great demand. Architects, builders, planners to locate the small farms and lay out plots, with deference to winds and climates. Biologists, chemists, for plant study and sewage hygiene. Aquatic polyculturists for pond designs. Waterworks construction designers and builders. Researchers in all areas. Livestock (including poultry) managers. Scientists of all kinds. Travel and trade specialists. And, yes, even politicians to work for the good of the community.

"A permaculture system integrated with human settlement provides an inexhaustible energy system, fueled by the sun and developed by the community," Mollison says. "I see no other solution to the problems of man than the formation of small responsible communities involved in Permaculture and appropriate technology."


We must each in our own way take stock of our portion of the spaceship. Check our own wasteful habits. Seek out alternatives in life-style, in energy use. As you plan your career, start thinking of the appropriate technology approach to the field you are interested in. You will want to explore further the new technologies we have discussed in the areas that appeal to you.

Then, all working together, from Loisaida to the San Joaquin Valley, we can build an appropriate future for our own small world.

# LIST OF SOURCES

BOOKS

Altshuler, Alan with Womack, James P. and Pucher, John R. *Urban Transportation System: Politics and Policy Innovation.* Cambridge, Mass.: MIT Press, 1979.

Bender, Tom. *Sharing Smaller Pies.* Portland, Ore.: RAIN, 1975.

Brainbridge, David A. *The First Passive Solar Catalogue.* Davis, Calif.: The Passive Solar Institute, 1980.

Brockington, Fraser. *World Health.* New York: Churchill Livingstone, 1975.

Bundy, Robert. (ed.) *Images of the Future: The Twenty-first Century and Beyond.* Buffalo, N.Y.: Prometheus Books, 1976.

Cahn, Robert. *Footprint on the Planet: A Search for an Environmental Ethic.* New York: Universe Books, 1978.

Carson, Rachel. *Silent Spring.* Boston: Houghton, Mifflin, 1962.

Coonley, Douglas R. *Wind: Making It Work for You.* Philadelphia: Franklin Institute Press, 1979.

Dickson, Paul. *The Future File: A Guide for People with One Foot in the 21st Century.* New York: Rawson Associates, 1977.

Dorf, Richard and Hunter, Yvonne. *Appropriate Visions.* San Francisco: Boyd & Fraser Publishing Co., 1978.

*Energy Primer: Solar, Water, Wind and Bio-Fuels.* Menlo Park, Calif.: Portola Institute, 1974.

Fischer, Stanley I. *Moving Millions.* New York: Harper & Row, 1979.

Gay, Larry. *The Complete Book of Heating with Wood.* Charlotte, Vt.: Garden Way Publishing Co., 1978.

Gofman, John W. and Tamplin, Arthur R. *Poisoned Power: The Case Against Nuclear Power Plants.* Emmaus, Pa.: Rodale Press, 1979.

Illich, Ivan. *Tools for Conviviality.* New York: Harper & Row, 1973.

Jeavons, John. *How to Grow More Vegetables: A Primer on the Life-Giving Bio-dynamic/French Intensive Method of Organic Horticulture.* Palo Alto, Calif.: Ecology Action of the Mid-Peninsula, 1974.

Kemp, Michael A., Kirby, Ronald F. *et al. Para-transit.* Washington, D.C.: Urban Institute, 1974.

*The Liklik Buk: A Rural Development Handbook for Papua New Guinea.* Lae, P.N.G.: The Melanesian Council of Churches, 1977.

Lincoln, John. *Methanol and Other Ways Around the Gas Pumps.* Charlotte, Vt.: Garden Way Publishing Co., 1976.

Lovins, Amory. *Soft Energy Paths: Towards a Durable Peace.* San Francisco: Friends of the Earth, 1977.

MEN Staff. *The Mother Earth News Handbook of Homemade Power.* New York: Bantam Books, 1974.

Mollison, Bill. *Permaculture II: Practical Design for Town and*

*Country in Permanent Agriculture*. Stanley, Tasmania, Australia: TAGARI Publishers, 1979.

*Producing Your Own Power: How to Make Nature's Energy Sources Work for You*. Emmaus, Pa.: Rodale Press, 1974.

*RAINbook: Resources for Appropriate Technology*. Portland, Ore.: RAIN, 1977.

Richards, Brian. *Moving in Cities*. Boulder, Col.: Westview Press, Inc., 1976.

Schneider, Stephen H. with Mesirow, Lynne E. *The Genesis Strategy: Climate and Global Survival*. New York: Plenum Publishing Co., 1979.

Schumacher, E. F. *Small Is Beautiful: Economics as if People Mattered*. New York: Harper & Row, 1973.

*Solar Gain: Winners of the Passive Solar Design Competition*. Sacramento: California Energy Commission, Publications Unit, 1980.

Thompson, William Irwin. *Darkness and Scattered Light*. Garden City, N.Y.: Anchor Press, 1978.

Tillman, David A. *Wood as an Energy Resource*. New York: Academic Press, Inc., 1978.

*The Village Handbook*. Cambridge, Md.: Volunteers in Technical Assistance (VITA), 1976.

Weigelt, Horst R., Gotz, Rainier E., and Weiss, Helmut H. *City Traffic*. New York: Van Nostrand Reinhold Co., 1973.

*Wind Power for Farms, Homes and Small Industry*. Springfield, Va.: National Technical Information Service, Dept. of Commerce.


## PERIODICALS

In the following magazines can be found the latest in ideas, inventions, and innovations of importance to those working with appropriate technology.

*AERO Sun-Times*, c/o Alternative Energy Resources Organization, 435 Stapleton Building, Billings, MT 59101.

*Alternate Currents,* c/o The Appropriate Technology Action Coalition, 156 Fifth Avenue, New York, NY 10010.

*Alternative Sources of Energy,* 107 South Central Avenue, Milaca, MN 56353.

*AT Newsletter,* c/o The Ohio Appropriate Technology Bulletin, Program for Energy Research, Education and Public Service, Ohio State University, 1712 Neil Avenue, Columbus, Ohio 43210.

*Cascade,* c/o Cascadian Regional Library, Box 1492, Eugene, OR 97401.

*Chemical Engineering,* McGraw-Hill, 1121 Avenue of the Americas, New York, NY 10020.

*Civil Engineering,* 345 East 47th Street, New York, NY 10017.

*Country Journal,* 139 Main Street, Brattleboro, VT 05301.

*Doing More with Less,* c/o Common Ground, 1090 South Adams, Birmingham, MI 48011.

*Ecology,* Duke University Press, Box 6697 College Station, Durham, NC 27708.

*Electric Vehicle News,* P. O. Box 533, Westport, CT 06880.

*Environment,* 4000 Albemarle Street, N.W., Washington, D. C. 20016.

*Flower and Garden,* 4251 Pennsylvania Avenue, Kansas City, MO 64111.

*The Futurist,* c/o The World Future Society, P. O. Box 30369, Bethesda Branch, Washington, D. C. 20014.

*Green Revolution,* P. O. Box 3233, York, PA 17402.

*Industrial Design,* 717 Fifth Avenue, New York, NY 10022.

*Intermediate Technology,* 556 Santa Cruz Avenue, Menlo Park, CA 94025.

*International Wildlife,* 8925 Leesburg Pike, Vienna, VA 22180.

*Journal of Soil and Water Conservation,* 7515 N.E. Ankeny Road, Ankeny, Iowa 50021.

*Living Alternatives,* P. O. Box 189, Newton, MA 02195.

*Mechanical Engineering,* 345 East 47th Street, New York, NY 10017.

*Mechanix Illustrated,* 1 Fawcett Place, Greenwich, CT 06830.

*Mid-Atlantic News*, c/o Citizens' Energy Project, 1110 6th Street, N.W., #300, Washington, D. C. 20001.

*The Mother Earth News*, P. O. Box 70, Hendersonville, NC 28791.

*New Age*, 32 Station Street, Brookline, MA 02146.

*New Roots*, c/o New England Appropriate Technology Network, P. O. Box 548, Greenfield, MA 01301.

*New Shelter*, Rodale Press, 33 E. Minor St., Emmaus, PA 18049.

*Organic Gardening*, Rodale Press, 33 E. Minor St., Emmaus, PA 18049.

*Popular Mechanics*, 224 West 57th Street, New York, NY 10019.

*Popular Science*, 380 Madison Avenue, New York, NY 10017.

*RAIN: Journal of Appropriate Technology*, c/o RAIN, 2270 N.W. Irving, Portland, OR 97210.

*Rural America*, c/o Center for Rural Affairs, 1346 Connecticut Ave. N.W., Washington, D. C. 20036.

*Soft Energy Notes*, c/o "Not Man Apart," newsletter, Friends of the Earth, 124 Spear Street, San Francisco, CA 94105.

*Solar Age*, P. O. Box 4934, Manchester, NH 03108.

*Solar Energy*, Pergamon Press, Maxwell House, Fairview Park, Elmsford, NY 10523.

*Tilth Newsletter*, Box 2382, Olympia, WA 98507.

*VITA News*, c/o Volunteers in Technical Assistance, 3706 Rhode Island Avenue, Mt. Rainier, MD 20822.

*The Workbook*, c/o Southwest Research & Information Center, P. O. Box 4524, Albuquerque, NM 87106.

For free catalogues, directories, and guidebooks on a variety of AT material and projects write to the following sources:

*Appropriate Community Technologies Sourcebook*, c/o Citizens' Energy Project, 1110 6th Street, N.W., Washington, D.C. 20001.

*Aquaculture Program Publications*, c/o Bodega Marine Laboratory, P. O. Box 247, Bodega Bay, CA 94923.

*Commercially Available Small Wind Systems and Equipment*,

c/o U. S. Department of Energy, Rocky Flats Wind Systems Programs, Box 464, Golden, CO 80401

*Design Alternatives, Inc.*, 1312 18th Street, N.W., Washington, D. C. 20036.

*The Hip-Pocket Urban Tree Planter*, c/o California Department of Forestry, 1416 Ninth Street, Sacramento, CA 95814.

*META Publications*, P. O. Box 128–T, Marble Mount, WA 98267.

*Northeast Yellow Pages of Free Solar Energy Resources*, c/o New England Solar Energy Association, P. O. Box 541, Brattleboro, VT 05301.

*Park Project Energy Interpretation*, National Recreation and Park Association, 1601 Kent Street, Arlington, VA 22209.

*Selected Federal Programs in Appropriate Technology*, c/o The Office of Technology Assessment, Panel on Appropriate Technology, Consumer Action Now, 355 Lexington Avenue, New York, NY 10017.

*Self-Reliance Newsletter*, c/o Institute for Local Self-Reliance, 1717 18th Street, N.W., Washington, D. C. 20009.

*TRANET*, The Transnational Network for Appropriate/Alternate Technologies, P. O. Box 567, Rangeley, Maine 04970.

*World AT Directory*, Organization for Economic Co-operation and Development (OECD), Director of Information, 2 rue Andre-Pascal 75775 Paris Cedex 16, France.


A partial listing of active AT organizations and agencies and their mailing addresses:


California Office of Appropriate Technology, 1530 10th Street, Sacramento, CA 95814.

Center for Community Economic Development, 1878 Massachusetts Avenue, Cambridge, MA 02140.

Clivus Multrum USA, 14–A Eliot Street, Cambridge, MA 02138.

Domestic Technology Institute, c/o Malcolm Lillywhite, Evergreen, CO 80439.

Ecotope, 747 15th Avenue East, Seattle, WA 98112.

Farallones Institute, c/o Bill & Helga Olkowski, P. O. Box 700, Point Reyes Station, CA 94956.

Institute for Local Self-Reliance, 1717 18th Street, N. W., Washington, D. C. 20009.

National Center for Appropriate Technology, P. O. Box 3838, Butte, MT 59701; Washington, D. C., office: c/o Scott Sklar, 815 15th Street, N.W., D. C. 20005.

The National Self-Help Resource Center, 2000 S Street, N.W., Washington, D. C., 20009.

New Alchemy Institute, Box 432, Woods Hole, MA 02540.

San Diego Center for Appropriate Technology, 5863 Hardy Avenue, San Diego, CA 92115.

U. S. Community Services Administration, 1200 19th Street, N.W., Washington, D. C., 20506.

U. S. Office of Technology Assessment, c/o U.S. Congress, Washington, D. C. 20510.

# INDEX

AFTER HIS early retirement from the interior design profession, Robert V. Doyle began a second career in free-lance writing. An introduction to the California Office of Appropriate Technology sent Mr. Doyle on an extensive investigation into career experiences, employment opportunities, and life within the growing AT community.

During his research, Mr. Doyle was deeply impressed by the AT message and the knowledgeable, sincere approach to the world's energy and environmental problems by scientists, inventors, entrepreneurs and philosophers who work and live "the AT way." This impression led to numerous articles and ultimately to his book, *Careers to Preserve Our Shrinking World: Working and Living with Appropriate Technology*.

Among other works, Mr. Doyle is author of *Your Career in Interior Design*. He and Mrs. Doyle live in Sacramento, California, where they are active in civic and community affairs.